Burning Issues

Ron Hutchinson is the author of *Says I, Says He*, winner of the George Devine Award (1978), *Eejits*, *The Irish Play*, *The Dillen*, *Rat in the Skull*, winner of the John Whiting Award (1984), an Olivier Award and a Critics' Circle Award in New York, Los Angeles and Chicago. His most recent stage work was a revival of *Rat in the Skull* (Royal Court, 1995) and an adaptation of Mikhail Bulgakov's *Flight* (Royal National Theatre, 1998). He lives in Los Angeles where he is an Emmy winning writer for television and features.

RON HUTCHINSON

Burning Issues

faber and faber

First published in 2000
by Faber and Faber Limited
3 Queen Square London WC1N 3AU

Published in the United States by Faber and Faber Inc.
An affiliate of Farrar, Straus and Giroux LLC, New York
Typeset by Faber and Faber Ltd
Printed in England by Mackays of Chatham plc, Chatham, Kent

All rights reserved

© Ron Hutchinson, 2000

Ron Hutchinson is hereby identified as author of this
work in accordance with Section 77 of the Copyright,
Designs and Patents Act 1988

All rights whatsoever in this play are strictly reserved. Application for
permission for any use whatsoever, including performance rights, must be
made in advance, prior to any such proposed use, to Judy Daish Associates
Ltd, 2 St Charles Place, London W10 6EG. No performance may be given
unless a licence has first been obtained

*This book is sold subject to the condition that it shall not, by way of trade
or otherwise, be lent, resold, hired out or otherwise circulated without the
publisher's prior consent in any form of binding or cover other than that
in which it is published and without a similar condition including this
condition being imposed on the subsequent purchaser*

A CIP record for this book
is available from the British Library

ISBN 0–571–20636–0

2 4 6 8 10 9 7 5 3 1

Characters

Alasdair Watkins
Edward Mallowan
Neil Brasher
Jessica Wright
Ben Richter
Hazeldene Blount

Burning Issues had its first performance, by arrangement with Michael Codron, at Hampstead Theatre (Artistic Director – Jenny Topper) on 25 April 2000. The cast was as follows:

Watkins William Chubb
Mallowan Kenneth Colley
Neil John Gordon-Sinclair
Jessica Miranda Pleasence
Richter Rob Spendlove
Hazeldene Andrew Woodall

Director Denis Lawson
Designer Anthony Ward
Lighting Howard Harrison
Sound Steve Brown

Act One

SCENE ONE

The lights rise and isolate Neil Brasher, sitting at a desk, reading aloud from a thick notebook in an educated, slightly sardonic Edinburgh accent.

Neil 'May the twentieth, 1992 –
 'Great perturbation in the street today. A family of darkies moved in to the end house, late the McGrovers, who did what used to be called a midnight flit. Tremendous concern all round. Will they slaughter chickens in the yard, roll their eyes and frighten the children?'

As he finds another entry in the book the lights slowly rise. By the time he's finished they'll reveal a high-tech conference room, in which he's at a sheet-metal desk with two other people.

'February the third, this year –
 '"Nigger", now. That's a word that really means what it says. Example. I came face to face with one in the High Street this afternoon. There was no other word for what he was but a Nigger. A man from Mars would have pointed at him and shouted "Nigger!" as he jumped back in alarm at seeing one for the first time.'

He closes the book and looks at the others in this publisher's office in one of the smarter media areas of London.
 They are Jessica Wright, an attractive, intense New Yorker in a business suit, and Hazeldene Blount, a pony-tailed middle-aged Englishman, dressed a little

too hiply for his age.

Jessica (*appalled*) Is every page like that?

Hazeldene Every entry?

Neil No, but at least once a week he lets fly. The Welsh come out pretty badly. And the Irish and the Scots. There's a very good joke about the Cornish somewhere.

Jessica The Jews?

He hands her the book.

Neil The sixteenth of July.

She reads it and sighs.

Jessica Oh my God.

Hazeldene Vicious libels or common abuse?

Neil Mostly abuse. Now and again some real bile comes through. I wouldn't put him down as a certifiable Nazi, but he'd give you a run for your money on the Protocols of the Elders of Zion.

Jessica hands Hazeldene the book and he flicks through it.

Neil On the brighter side, the Faroese don't seem to be mentioned and he doesn't go out of his way to insult anyone from Goa –

Hazeldene There's no way to make light of this, Neil.

Neil That was babbling, Hazeldene. Authentic babbling.

Jessica Is this the only volume?

Neil There are six more in my flat, 1967 to 1999.

Hazeldene Your flat? Lying there, in your flat?

Neil What should I have done with them?

Hazeldene Don't bring them here. You should rent a safe deposit box.

What are you doing about it?

Neil I phoned Watkins last night – he's visiting professor somewhere in California.

I kept it vague – asked about the journals in a roundabout way, if he'd ever seen them when working on the biography, how forthcoming Mallowan had been, etc.

He swears Mallowan told him point blank he didn't keep a journal.

Jessica He took him at his word?

Neil Watkins is an academic, not a crime reporter.

Hazeldene I always had my doubts about Watkins.

Neil He came up with that stuff on who Mallowan's real father was, didn't he? Everybody else missed that in all the thousands of words Mallowan's had written about him.

Hazeldene Even so, I always had the sense that Watkins was a little – wobbly.

Jessica I always wanted LeFèvre, that's no secret.

Neil LeFèvre is a demolition expert. You call him in when you want some tottering ruin of a literary reputation finally exploded. An entire new generation of readers is finding Mallowan – and making a not inconsiderable amount of money for this firm in the process.

Hazeldene Rather gone and cut his own throat now, hasn't he? (*He hands the journal back to Neil and heads to the door with a tight smile.*) Don't go away, you two.

The door closes, leaving Neil and Jessica alone.

Neil (*bitter, quoting*) I always wanted LeFèvre.

Ignoring him, Jessica dials.

Jessica (*on phone, in Italian*) Nino – we'll be coming over this Friday for four or five days –

Neil (*warning*) We're all going to hang together on this.

Jessica (*on phone, in Italian*) It'll be Mr Neil and myself – just the two of us, no guests this time –

Neil I'm not carrying the can.

Jessica (*on phone, in Italian*) You'll need to send the car to the airport at six. Six o'clock, make sure the car is there this time –

Neil Bloody Watkins. How in God's name could he have missed the journals?

Jessica (*on phone, in Italian*) The water? There can't be trouble with the water again, we had everything replaced before the summer began –

Neil Bugger Mallowan. Bugger bugger bugger.

Jessica sets the phone down.

Jessica Nino says there's no water coming out of the taps, just a brown sludge.

Neil We replaced the pipes.

Jessica On the other hand, the olives are doing well.

Neil I should sit down and figure exactly how many tens of thousands of pounds each bottle of olive oil costs me every year.

Jessica Us. Costs us.

Frustrated, Neil kicks the waste basket across the room.

Neil I take an author the firm's had on the books for years without anything to show for it. I develop a relationship with him – one of the most difficult, evasive men of letters in the business, in a business where being a slippery wee shit is an art form. I put his bio on the non-fiction bestseller list for ten straight weeks –

Jessica And you make a splashy announcement that we're going to publish his journals without having the sense to read the damn things first.

Now it turns out they could fit nicely on the shelf next to Hitler's *Table Talk*.

Neil It's not just the Jews, he doesn't like anybody. What's even more depressing than the force with which he expresses his opinions is their banality.

You'd think that if one of the giants of European literature was to descend to racist abuse, at the least it could be original and well written. He owes us that much, doesn't he?

Jessica It's a bloody mess.

Neil And it's *our* mess. Let none of us forget that.

The lights snap out and rise on:

SCENE TWO

Richter's office, where Richter, an American, with close-cropped hair and outdoorsman tan, is exercising on a rowing machine, sleeves rolled up, shirt unbuttoned. He looks up at Hazeldene, continuing to row as they talk.

Hazeldene I know you're still settling in, getting your feet wet, but something's cropped up on the Mallowan front.

Richter Mallowan?

Hazeldene *The Hotel Lucerne, A History of Hell* – he's been on our list for years. Edward Mason Mallowan. A steady seller, nothing spectacular, but we had a real lift-off last year with his biography.

We intended following up the success of *The Gloomy Englishman* by publishing his journals.

Richter *The Gloomy* –?

Hazeldene Last season's biggest hit for the Non-Fiction division. Alasdair Watkins's bio.

Richter Of –?

Hazeldene Of Mallowan.

Richter Mallowan, right. Wasn't there an announcement?

Hazeldene moves his balance from left leg to right leg and back to keep up with Richter's movement on the exercise machine.

Hazeldene A party was thrown, yes. I thought it was a little premature but Neil was eager to stake out Mallowan as ours – perhaps a soupçon over-eager.

Richter Neil?

Hazeldene Neil Brasher.

Richter Brasher, yes, the Irishman.

Hazeldene Scot.

Richter Shouldn't you be taking this up with Legal?

Hazeldene It's not that kind of problem. Neil – whose baby this really is – assures me that all the geese are in a row –

Richter Ducks.

Hazeldene (*ignoring him*) – but there's a question of what the journal entries reveal about Mallowan.

Richter Little boys?

Hazeldene No.

Richter Little girls? Big boys and big girls, all together in one bed?

Hazeldene Race.
  Blacks, Asians, Jews, the Irish – over the years he's devoted entire swathes of his journals to them. Watkins – never my first choice – managed to produce three hundred and sixteen pages about his subject without once suspecting it.

Richter We're screwed?

Hazeldene There's a deal letter. Neil and Jessica insisted we move fast to lock up the rights.

Richter Jessica? The copy-editor Sedgewick found in New York?

Hazeldene She's a commissioning editor now. Based here.

Richter Is Sedgewick out of the mental home yet?

Hazeldene He had it pretty bad but I think he's back with his wife and children now. And his hair's started to grow again.

Richter Who inherited her?

Hazeldene Professionally or personally?

Richter Both.

Hazeldene Neil, both.

Richter Any more bad news?

Hazeldene Mallowan writes very slowly. His last book was nine years ago. He's been working on his next at his usual glacier pace. Three months ago he said something which seemed to imply that he was within sight of The End – give or take a few geological aeons.

It'll be a major literary event. Not to mention a marketing bonanza. Unfortunately, he's free to take it anywhere he chooses.

Richter gets off the machine.

Richter Three minutes. Mallowan. Highlights. Major topological features. Places of interest.

He gets dressed for business again as the book jacket of The Gloomy Englishman *is projected on the wall. It shows the sixty-year-old Mallowan in a black-and-white photograph.*

He's been caught on the street, in a mackintosh and flat cap, in a neighbourhood of dreary Victorian terraced houses on an overcast, northern day.

A plastic shopping bag is in his hand and he looks like any senior citizen on his way home from the local supermarket – there's nothing about him to suggest genius or literary involvement.

Hazeldene *The Hotel Lucerne* was Mallowan's first novel.

In 1939 the Nazis put up for auction a lot of the art work they'd labelled degenerate. The protagonist of the novel is the son of a banned artist. He pleads with one of the potential buyers not to bid. He'd rather his father's life work be destroyed than contribute in any way to the Third Reich. The art dealer refuses. The art works in question belong to the world. To destroy them will give the Nazis an even bigger victory.

Richter What does he do?

Hazeldene The novel has two endings. In one of them he leaves Lucerne without the paintings. They're destroyed. When the artist hears of it in Dachau he kills himself. His life meant nothing.

In the second ending the dealer buys them. We follow

the money raised back to Germany. It pays for the gas chamber Siemens builds that kills most of the members of the art dealer's family.

In Mallowan's world, you see, moral decisions are shown for what they are – literature. We go to them thinking we'll find some mathematical truth in them – we never do. It perplexed him all his life. It's all he ever wrote about.

You see how astonishing it is, how – to be fair to Neil and Jessica and Watkins – how totally unexpected it is that the Mallowan who writes of such a perplexing and profound moral issue – who in all his books finds a complex ethical dilemma to explore – can also be the author of the journals.

Richter But he's good, is he?

Hazeldene Oh yes.

Richter Great?

Hazeldene Well now, who reads John O'Hara these days or Compton Mackenzie, but in their day –

Richter Is he a great writer?

Hazeldene We'll know for sure in thirty years –

Richter (*impatient*) How great a writer is he?

Hazeldene The French and Scandinavians love him. His sales in German are extraordinary. He's a cult figure in Japan. This next one – the Nobel wouldn't be out of the question.

Richter The Irishman – Shaney?

Hazeldene Heaney. Seamus Heaney. That was for poetry and being Irish doesn't count.

Richter How many titles in the back list?

Hazeldene Six – all in print, all fizzing like rockets since the bio.

Richter But at night the guy dresses up in a storm-trooper's uniform?

Hazeldene He's a little right of centre you might say, yes.

Richter Couldn't be a joke? The journals?

Hazeldene Mallowan isn't noted for rib-ticklers.

Richter I always thought your scandals were sexual. Vicars and schoolgirls, Boy Scouts and Members of Parliament.

Hazeldene We could handle that.

Richter Might even put a little English on the sales.

Hazeldene Spin. We say spin.

Richter reaches for his tie and knots it.

Richter Conference room. Five minutes. I want everybody in there who's connected with this. (*He slams his fist into his palm.*) Get me? We're going to span the watershed.

As Hazeldene heads away lights go out and rise on:

SCENE THREE

The conference room, where Jessica is alone, reading through the journal, making notes. She looks up as Hazeldene enters.

Jessica Did Richter know who Mallowan is?

Hazeldene No, but he faked it pretty well. Sorry – pretty good.
  Neil?

Jessica Legal. Looking for wriggle room in the deal letter.

Shakily, Hazeldene pours himself some water from the carafe on the table.

Hazeldene I used to work with someone who survived all the purges and takeovers in the publishing world by disconnecting his phone and entering and leaving his office via the window. His theory was that if he stayed out of the corridor and was never seen at meetings, he'd get by.

He dropped his guard one day and went for a pee and was fired while shaking his willy dry. (*He punches his fist into his palm.*) We're going to span the watershed. Five minutes. When Richter gets here.

Jessica What are you talking about?

Hazeldene Richter just said it. You're American, too.

Jessica It'll be some business-school thing. Don't worry about it.

An explosive sigh from Hazledene.

Hazeldene My boat. That's what I live for now. All this crap gets put in its place when you're shipping it green and looking a thirty-foot wave in the eye over the foredeck.

Jessica Yo ho ho, but we're in this together, you, me and Neil. You signed off on publishing the journals, remember?

Hazeldene Sod the journals. (*He stares at the journals as if they're toxic.*) There's something not quite right about anyone who keeps a journal past the age of puberty, don't you think?

Jessica Like locking yourself in your study and jerking off?

Hazeldene (*automatic*) Wanking.
A solitary vice.

Jessica Masturbation?

Hazeldene Keeping a journal.
Anything about us in there? The firm?

Jessica There's one passage where he describes your laugh in very unflattering terms.

Hazeldene (*stiffly*) Excise the personal insults and the racist rants, what's left?

Jessica Complaints about the weather, the quality of dry-cleaning, how little there is on television that's worth watching, and data on the frequency and firmness of his bowel movements.

Hazeldene (*bewildered*) This from the author of *The Hotel Lucerne*? (*He checks that the door is closed.*) Why don't we let Neil take care of this one himself? (*He moves closer to her.*) I know you've seen him as the coming man here but I always thought there was something of the doomed quality of, say, Sedgewick about him. (*He moves forward again so that his body is against hers.*) And we all know how Sedgewick ended up –

The door opens and Richter enters. Hazeldene picks up the journal.

The first volume. Neil has the others. I've impressed on him how important their physical security is.

Richter puts his hands behind his back, refusing even to touch it.

Richter How bad is it?

Jessica He doesn't have a good word for anyone unless they're English – and even then the words 'thieving

Cockney gits' suggest his toleration for his fellow Englishmen isn't universal.

Hazeldene It goes without saying he's an anti-Semite of the worst sort, too.

Neil's at the door; he has overheard.

Neil What exactly would an anti-Semite of the better sort be?

Hazeldene You know what I mean. You should do, Neil, you brought the damn journals to us.

Neil Perhaps we're panicking. There are all those questions about Eliot. They haven't interfered with his reputation as a poet. Ezra Pound is still read, isn't he? Orwell said that if the force of belief behind it is strong enough, any worldview which only just passes the test of sanity is sufficient to produce a work of art. Take *Bambi* –

Richter *Bambi?*

Neil The author of the original book was one of Austria's pre-eminent pornographers.

Richter What are you talking about?

Jessica You're babbling again, Neil.

Neil I am, yes.

Hazeldene Are you suggesting we plough ahead and publish?

Neil Legal says we're screwed if we don't. Not that I went into the gory details, just told them something had come up.

Hazeldene (*insistent, to Jessica*) What do you think? Is that your position too, Jessica?

Jessica I think – I think we should figure how to span the watershed on this. That's what I think.

Richter grunts assent, takes charge, pulling the blinds down and barking an order into the speakerphone.

Richter No calls. (*He turns to them, ready for action.*) Anybody outside of this room know we have the journals?

Neil It's just Jessica, Hazeldene, you, me.

Richter You three will handle this. I will advise, informally. All discussions will be verbal, nothing will be put in writing.

Someone has to sound Mallowan out, see how committed he is to having the damn things published. That's going to be you, Neil, isn't it?

Neil That would be a very bad idea.

Hazeldene He's your tar baby.

Neil I shepherded the biography, it's true, but I never met him personally.

Richter Never?

Neil I did all the negotiations by phone. That's how he wanted it. He guards his privacy, lives in the same house he lived in when he was an insurance clerk, in this small mill town on the edge of nowhere. Never sees anyone. (*A bland smile at Hazeldene.*) Of course, if Hazeldene's feeling is that I should handle things I'll do it, but I can't guarantee they'll go well.

Richter Hazeldene? You've had dealings with him?

Hazeldene Not face to face, as it were.

Richter You could handle him, though?

Hazeldene stares grimly at Neil.

Hazeldene He wouldn't be the first awkward bugger I've seen off but I'm not sure that my relationship with him is any more solid than Neil's.

Jessica There's a slighting reference to Hazeldene in one of the entries.

Neil reads the entry she's flagged.

Neil 'A giggle like an obsequious eunuch at the court of a minor debauchee.' (*He snorts with laughter.*) 'Minor debauchee' – that's very good.

Richter (*impatient*) Jessica?

Jessica Anything, Richter, but – an American? For a job like this? Now that we know what he thinks of us?

Richter Then it's Watkins. I presume the biography was reasonably sympathetic or Mallowan wouldn't have trusted us with his journals?

Neil pours himself water from the carafe on the table.

Neil I chose Watkins exactly because he'd do a fair-minded, balanced, *workmanlike* job. There was a camp in the firm pushing for someone edgier, flashier, like, well, LeFèvre, but while I concede LeFèvre's brilliance, he might have decided it was his own reputation for vigorous use of the wrecking ball that was at stake here and not Mallowan's literary one.

With Alasdair Watkins we got what we wanted – more importantly, what Mallowan wanted, as much as one can ever tell what that is.

At the end of the day he did an admirable job for us and I've no reason to believe he pissed Mallowan off doing it.

Richter He missed the journals.

Neil Yes, well, I'd agree he's not quite in the top flight. Not exactly Premier League.

Hazeldene (*needling*) You would think that a professional biographer might, at some point, ask his subject if he keeps a journal?

Neil Mallowan lied point blank. Watkins is adamant.

Richter You couldn't have let sleeping dogs lie? Said thanks but no thanks when Mallowan offered you the journals?

Neil No offence, Ben, but Mallowan is important. He's big. I came into the profession under the spell of writers like Mann, Grass, Faulkner. Mallowan is such a writer. That may not mean much to the bean-counters who more and more run this industry but, by God, it matters to me.

Richter (*grimly*) This firm hadn't made a profit in fifteen years when we took it over. Nobody would be reading anything of anybody unless somebody was counting the beans.

You have Watkins's number?

Neil Yes.

Richter Get him here.

Neil The time difference?

Richter *Get him*.

As Neil dials, Hazeldene edges closer to Richter.

Hazeldene Watkins never was my idea. I hope that's clear. Watkins? I mean to say – *Watkins*.

Neil gets through.

Neil (*on phone*) Alasdair? Neil here, sorry to get you out of bed –

No, I didn't see the reviews in the *University of Saskatoon Journal,* you must send me a copy –
A copy of all the reviews you've been putting together? – Yes – a spiral binder sounds just the thing –
No, nothing on the Spanish-language rights. Yes – I do agree there are a lot of Spanish speakers in the world –

Jessica moves closer to Richter.

Jessica Watkins. I mean – Watkins?

Richter (*puzzled*) Yes?

Jessica That's all. *Watkins.*

She turns away. Neil is still trying to get a word in on the phone.

Neil (*on phone*) I think we all feel that about Accounting and how slow they are –
It is a lot of money, I agree – well, it isn't a lot of money but it is the principle – no, I'm not saying it isn't a lot of money – it won't be possible to put you through to Accounting, it's rather late in the day and that isn't the purpose of –
I'm making a note. I'll take it to them first thing tomorrow –
Why not now? – Yes, I could do that, I could place a note on their door before I leave tonight –

He swings round to see Richter looking grimly at him; Hazeldene smiling cheerfully at his discomfort and Jessica rolling her eyes.

Neil (*on phone*) Don't hang up –

Richter grabs another phone.

Richter (*on phone*) Ben Richter here. Vice-President, Publishing, Europe.
I want you on a plane, tonight, first thing tomorrow,

whenever –

Emboldened, Hazeldene picks up a phone also.

Hazeldene (*on phone*) Hazeldene here. Now listen –

Richter (*on phone*) Planes leave Los Angeles every hour of the day and night, I know, I've seen them.

Hazeldene (*on phone*) This isn't the time to quibble over first class or business –

Beside herself at being out of the loop, Jessica hisses to Neil.

Jessica Give me the phone.

Neil You want to beat up on him, too? (*He shields it from her grasp. On phone*) No, that isn't the way we usually talk to our writers, Alasdair, but Hazeldene's a little panicked at the moment.

Jessica takes out her cell phone, looks up the number in Neil's address book and dials.

Richter (*on phone*) LAX to Heathrow, Heathrow to Manchester, we'll have somebody waiting there for you. In fact, we'll all be there.

Hazeldene (*on phone*) Manchester, yes, you're going to be seeing Mallowan. We can't go into it on the phone but something's turned up.

Neil (*on phone*) It's bad, Alasdair, really bad – in fact, really really really really bad –

Jessica gets through on the cell phone.

Jessica (*on phone*) Alasdair, it's Jessica here, Jessica Wright –
  Yes, I know you're on the other line to Richter, Hazeldene and Neil –

The others stare at her, phones in their hands as she takes over.

I'm with them in the office and whatever your feelings about having to pay for your own air ticket up front and being spoken to like that, I seriously advise you for the sake of your writing and academic careers to cut the crap and get your ass on a plane within the hour –
No one's interested –
I said no one's interested –
Bring it up when you get here –
Just do it, okay?

She smiles sweetly at the others as they set their phones back on the rest.

Okay, Ben?

The lights snap out and go up on:

SCENE FOUR

Manchester hotel suite, where trays of dirty plates and coffee cups are piled against a closed interior door, which leads to Watkins's bedroom. Richter, fretful and impatient, is waiting in the living area. The door to the corridor is ajar.
  Richter is about to knock on the door, thinks better of it, turns away as Jessica enters.

Richter What took so long?

Jessica The problem with making us all travel separately to Manchester and having Watkins check in under an assumed name is that it's very difficult to locate which room anyone is in. You do see that?

Richter Security.

At the height of our takeover battle for Penn, Sneddon and Arps I slept in a different hotel room every night for three weeks.

Jessica (*sweetly*) Couldn't find one you liked? (*She turns away, looks at the door.*) How long has he been in there?

Richter All night.

Jessica Christ.

Richter He's got all seven volumes and Mallowan's handwriting is lousy. (*He impatiently drums his fingers on the door jamb.*) How's your room?

Jessica I lifted up my blanket, there was a huge brown stain as if a horse had bled to death on it. Apart from that –

Richter Apart from that I should be in Frankfurt right now.

Jessica I should be in Tuscany.

Richter The Hamptons of Europe.

Jessica All the people you spend your business life trying to get away from on your doorstep.
You have a place in the Hamptons?

Richter Seven thousand square foot. *Architectural Digest*, April this year.
Concorde, we could be there for supper.
If this asshole ever finishes.

The lights rise on the bedroom behind the still-closed door. Watkins is sitting slumped at a small table beside the bed.

He's a tall, gangling, bespectacled and awkward Englishman, half dead with jet lag. The journals are piled in front of him. His head is in his hands. He gives a little moan.

In the living area Richter stares at the door, as if he heard the sound, then turns back to Jessica.

Richter Yale, spring semester, 1992. (*looking at Jessica*) You had a little thing with Watkins when he was teaching your final year. It's the reason you didn't want him here. The reason you didn't want him to get the bio in the first place.

Jessica Nice work. (*recovering*) It wasn't personal. I just didn't think he was good enough. On the other hand, at least he's safe.

Richter Safe?

Jessica In some ways his sheer incompetence has much to recommend it. The journals are still a secret, aren't they? (*She lets it sink in.*) Which Hampton?

Richter East. Acabonic Bay. On the water. You can see Jackson Pollock's painting barn from the front window. (*thinking it over*) Yes, they are, aren't they?

Hazeldene enters, flustered, edgy and out of breath.

Hazeldene Of course the problem with not knowing which name Watkins is booked in under means that one has to walk every floor, one at a time, to find the bugger.

Jessica I pointed that out.

Hazeldene (*indicates the door*) He's in there?

Richter (*nods*) You covered your tracks?

Hazeldene I've put it around that I'm on my boat and out of touch until Monday.

Richter Jessica?

Jessica Tuscany. With the phone off the hook.

Hazeldene How long has he –?

Jessica All night.

Hazeldene If he'd been half as thorough in the three years he was working on the book –

> *In the bedroom Watkins gets to his feet. He contorts his face into a savage grimace and gives a two-fingered sign and other obscene gestures to the journals.*
> *In the living area Hazeldene turns to Jessica.*

Did Neil speak to Mallowan?

Jessica He's having trouble getting through.

Richter Hasn't gone round in person?

Hazeldene Mallowan hates that.

Richter Couldn't have taken him by surprise? A flanking movement?

Jessica Mallowan can see you coming for miles, apparently. A German TV crew came to interview him after he won some literary prize. Refused to open the door.

Hazeldene Just as well. Might have called them 'bloody Krauts' on camera and there goes the Nobel.

Richter What?

Hazeldene Bloody Krauts. It's an expression.

> *His grin goes as he sees how angry Richter has suddenly become.*

Richter I know most of you think that because I come from the other side of this business I can't read or write but I read four hundred pages of *The Hotel Lucerne* last night and on the plane up here. I don't know if I can finish the other three hundred pages because I find it too painful and personal.

My grandfather's art collection was looted by the

'bloody Krauts' before the war. From time to time pieces come on the market. There's a Corot we've traced to a dealer in Frankfurt, he may have the rest of it – a couple of Van Eycks, a Goya.

It's not their money value, it's what they represent.

I don't know what the hell to make of Mallowan's journals but I know what's in the novel and it's pretty damn on the mark and you'd better start giving a rat's ass about the situation you've helped put us in as his publishers.

Hazeldene (*in shock*) I'd no idea –

Richter But now you have, you've got it?

Hazeldene (*swallowing*) Got it.

Richter You're sure about that? Because if you're not, if you don't think this is serious, if you can only deal with it at your usual arm's length as if there's nothing that's worth a good God damn, you can get on a plane back to London now.

Hazeldene Got it, Richter, got it. Understood. Message received.

Jessica (*puzzled, to Richter*) Are you defending the journals? Now you know what they say?

Richter's instinct for self-preservation kicks in.

Richter I don't know what they say. I know what you tell me they say. I've no intention of reading them.

Neil hurries in, frustrated and ill-tempered.

Neil You see, Ben, if you don't allow people to know what room you've booked yourself in to, it makes things a little complicated when they have to find you –

Jessica Drop it.

Neil detects the warning note in her voice, looks at the door.

Neil This is him, we're sure?

In the bedroom Watkins opens the small refrigerator beside the table. He takes out every single one of the spirit miniatures and pours them into a glass.
In the living area Richter snaps a question to Neil.

Richter Did you get through to Mallowan?

Hazeldene Will he see him?

Neil (*evasive*) I called.

Richter Does he know what it's about?

Neil (*even more evasive*) I mentioned the journals but it's probably better to let Watkins choose his moment.

Richter But he will see him?

Neil (*carefully*) I did call.

In the bedroom Watkins swishes the drinks around, then swallows it in one.
Hazeldene smells a rat.

Hazeldene We've been hanging on by a thread as serious publishers since the firm was taken over. Mallowan saved our bacon last season. We don't have anything for this one except these bloody journals. Has he agreed to see Watkins or hasn't he?

Neil What bloody use would it be even if he had? What's Mallowan going to say? It was all a joke?

Hazeldene So he hasn't?

Jessica Oh my God.

Neil He didn't even seem to remember who Watkins was.

Kept asking if he was from the Gas Board. Now I know better than anyone how difficult Mallowan can be –

Unseen by them, the door to the bedroom opens and Watkins comes out, ready to face to music.

But you'd have to say there's something memorably unmemorable about poor old Alasdair. That shambling, apologetic facelessness, that don't-mind-me-ness and his professorial stoop are some of the reasons I chose him –

Jessica is the first to see Watkins.

Jessica (*warning*) Neil –

Neil (*persisting*) They're exactly the qualities needed to reassure a wily old sod like Mallowan that you're not out to do him in – but those very qualities are exactly the ones which may have made him, in Mallowan's recollection, disappear up his own fundament –

Hazeldene now sees Watkins.

Hazeldene Neil –

Neil (*in full flow, as if getting it off his chest*) Where I should like to stick the journals the gormless twerp forgot – *forgot* – in the name of the Holy Mother of God – forgot to ask about of the man whose biography he was writing – (*He turns and sees Watkins.*) Alasdair –

Watkins Neil.

Neil strides past him and picks up the journals. He waves them about, as if he's on the verge of a crack-up.

Neil Journals? Journals? What bloody journals?

The lights snap out and rise on:

SCENE FIVE

Mallowan's study.

Books and newspaper cuttings are piled all around as the sixty-year-old Mallowan stands at the door, facing out.

Unused to visitors and company, Mallowan seems preoccupied and fretful, with erratic pauses in his speech. Now and again some sly and some not so sly malice comes through his vague, bookish demeanour.

His accent reveals someone who's never been outside of the few squares miles of his home town – a flat, northern, no-nonsense accent which sometimes tails off into querulousness.

Watkins is at the door, through which Mallowan seems reluctant to let him step.

Mallowan I told O'Halloran – all deliveries through the back door.

Watkins I'm Watkins.

Someone starts banging in the rear of the house. Mallowan raises his voice above it.

Mallowan Is it about the water heater?

Watkins also raises his voice as a dog starts barking furiously, offstage.

Watkins Alasdair Watkins. It's about the journals –

Mallowan cups his ear, shouts back.

Mallowan The Gas Board?

The noise suddenly subsides.

Watkins *The Gloomy Englishman.* Didn't Neil speak to you? Neil Brasher? Your publisher? He didn't tell you I was coming?

He slips through the door, into the room, as the banging, hammering and howling start up again. Mallowan looks at him with a jaundiced eye, reluctantly closes the door.

Mallowan Can't make it too long. They'll be needing to take the floor up in here. Started when I couldn't get the bathroom to flush. Cut a long story short, some tree roots had got into the drain. Water, see, they head for water. Once they get in, there's nothing you can do about it. They start to follow the drains into the house. Before you know it, they've cracked them open – cast iron here, you see, pre-war, First War at that, likely – and then you're truly buggered. Whole lot had to come out, floors up, everything.

The noise starts again. The banging ends as suddenly as it began but the howling continues.

Said to myself – seeing as they're here, why not get the whole shooting match seen to, put a new immersion and gas heater in.

Who are you, again?

Watkins Watkins. The biography. (*He holds up the copy he's carrying.*)

Mallowan What about it?

Watkins I wrote it.

The dog keeps barking somewhere in the back of the house.

Mallowan Not mine. Mrs Harris's dog, the housekeeper. You remember her? Large woman, red hands. She's away for two weeks seeing her sister in Sheffield, couldn't manage the dog, would I mind?

Watkins You're still happy here?

Mallowan stares around the room as if he'd never seen it before.

Mallowan Here? Well, I've been here –

Watkins (*promptly*) Forty-five years. Forty-six in November. The eleventh.

Mallowan That long? Well, like Larkin said about Hull – I don't suppose I'd be any happier or any more miserable anywhere else.

More banging and howling as Mallowan reaches for something on his desk.

Watkins, right –
 I've got something for you now you're here –

As he roots through the papers a sheaf of manuscript paper falls to the floor and Watkins gets on his hands and knees to pick it up.

Now then – (*He jabs his thumb at one of the sheets.*) Page nine, line sixteen – my father's car was a Wolseley, not an Austin, that was a very important distinction in those days; page twelve, fifth line, Arnold was my maternal, not my paternal uncle; page thirteen, line nine, my father worked in Sundry Accounts for Manchester Corporation, not Accounting –

An awestruck Watkins is staring at the papers in his hand.

Watkins Is this it? Your next novel?

Mallowan (*ignoring it*) Page fifteen, line three –

Watkins is still holding the manuscript as if it's something holy.

Watkins This is the final novel in *The Hotel Lucerne* sequence?

Mallowan (*impatient*) Do you want to hear the list or don't you?

Watkins reluctantly sets the manuscript down but can't resist shooting looks at it from time to time.

Watkins The journals – they're why I'm here –

Mallowan You'll be editing them?

Watkins That was the plan until –

Mallowan (*fretful*) Coming up here again, week after week, asking questions, wanting to know what I think about things, what I remember?
Oh dear, oh dear –
It's not that I mind you, not personally, but it's such a distraction. I'd never have agreed to any of it if I'd known what I was letting myself in for.

Watkins is slightly nettled.

Watkins I never did entirely understand why you authorized the biography in the first place. You weren't particularly, well – helpful.

Mallowan If I hadn't said yes that Scotsman would have gone ahead anyway.

Watkins Brasher?

Mallowan '*There is no sight in nature more awesome than that of a Scotsman on the make.*' J. M. Barrie.
Had to look out for myself. Until I'd got this under my belt, anyway. (*He picks up the manuscript of the novel.*) Never thought when I started out it'd take me ten novels to finish the bugger.

Watkins Twelve. Twelve including the novellas. When did you finish?

Mallowan Last night. I thought I'd try my hand at a

short story now.

Watkins You're writing again? So soon?

Mallowan '*Does a cobbler wait for inspiration before starting on another pair of boots?*' Trollope. (*He pours himself a cup of tea with the fussy movements of a lifelong bachelor.*) I was having a cuppa when you threw yourself through the door –

Watkins I'll make this as quick as I can.

Mallowan You won't mind if I don't offer you one?

Watkins The journals –

Mallowan I know what you're going to say. Not totally interesting, no. It's not as if I'd had what you might call a large life. I mean, just take a look around, it says it all, doesn't it?

But once you feel comfortable in a place, or, at any rate, not that uncomfortable, it's so hard to leave, don't you find?

It confounds me why anybody would think they're in the slightest worth publishing but there you are. (*He tips a pile of unopened letters out of a shoebox on his desk.*) Last month's mail. Fan letters, begging letters, *Dear Mr Mallowan this, Dear Mr Mallowan that, I'm writing a thesis, I wonder if you could explain* – (*Agitated*) They come to my door, you know. Follow me to the shops, gawping, taking snaps. Publishing the journals, telling them what a small, uninteresting life I actually lead might get them off my neck, and there's always the advance –

Watkins The advance?

Mallowan leans forward, lowers his voice.

Mallowan It'll put a new roof on and I can do all the

gutters before next winter. My down spouts aren't worth a light.

Watkins tries to assert some control over the interview.

Watkins You told me to my face you didn't keep a journal.

Mallowan I'd been reading Cesare Pavese. He said no man with an intimation of immortality would ever admit to it. (*A malicious little chuckle.*) Anyroad, I couldn't make it too easy for you, could I? Wasn't it your job to find them? I mean, you're like some bugger who breaks in with a six-shooter asking where the goods are.

Watkins (*stiffly*) I didn't see my role as that, exactly.

Mallowan (*waspishly*) What were you then? A collaborator? In some work of fiction that happened to be my life?

Watkins I assumed – foolishly, it's clear – that there was some tacit understanding between a biographer and his subject –

Mallowan Like between a man with a gun and the man with the goods?

Watkins This was an authorized biography, not a ram raid. I'm a fan, it was almost an act of piety to walk around the house you grew up in and the school you went to, not to mention wait outside the door for hours until you decided to answer it.

Chuckling, Mallowan unlocks a biscuit barrel, takes a custard cream out, locks the barrel and eats it.

Mallowan I'm not used to folk. Especially not when they're flipping notebooks in my face.

Watkins I think I discharged my duty to you. To listen, to record, to make as few judgements as I could and let the facts of your life speak for themselves –

Mallowan Facts? Of a life? What did Nabokov say? '*The truth is threefold. Shaped by the teller, re-shaped by the listener and the truth concealed from both by the dead man of the tale.*'

I'd offer you a custard cream only I'm right out.

Watkins You were not a dead man. You sat there nodding, occasionally grunting yes or no, you didn't even stop me when I began to pursue my ideas on the relationship between Great-Uncle Bob and your mother –

Trying to control himself, Watkins flips through sample pages in the journals he's brought with him.

Darkies. Coons. Niggers. Paddies. Wogs. Wops. Jungle Bunnies. Taffs. Camel Jockeys. Rag Heads. Eye-Ties. Square Heads. Kikes –

My God. I mean – my God.

Mallowan opens his mouth but Watkins keeps speaking.

Ten novels, two novellas, each of them an ethical debate between living, breathing human beings, a moral universe peopled by some of the most extraordinary characters in twentieth-century fiction, brought, no doubt, to a triumphant conclusion in that – (*He reaches hungrily at the new manuscript again, forces himself to keep his hands off it.*) If one wanted a road map to the horrors of the times of ourselves, our fathers and grandfathers, one would turn to Mallowan, the master of both great themes and domestic detail and yet – and yet – the maker of this world that seems to contain in it all the pain and suffering and moral confusions of our time writes about –

Temporarily out of words, he gestures at the journals. Mallowan picks up the errata sheet.

Mallowan When you're ready – page twenty, line seven,

my dad's brother lost his left leg in the First War, not his right –

Watkins persists.

Watkins How – how can the journals – the journals which you deliberately concealed from me – be filled with *darkies* when none of the characters in any of your novels talk like this?

Mallowan I don't suppose they do.

Watkins You could read every word of them and not be aware that's what you really feel.

Mallowan (*offhand*) They're novels. I make them up.

Watkins Don't they contain the truth about you?

Mallowan Why should you think that?

Watkins What you write in the journals is really what you feel?

Mallowan It's a sight more likely to be, isn't it?

Watkins You could read every word of the biography and not realize it.

Mallowan I noticed that. (*turning back to the list of errata*) Now, page twenty one, line two –

Watkins You kept it from me –

Mallowan I didn't keep anything from you. I didn't think they were all that interesting. I thought my work was what counted, not what I had for breakfast.

Watkins You didn't conceal them because of what they reveal about you?

Mallowan We all feel that way about darkies around here, ask anyone.

For a moment Watkins nearly loses it.

Watkins You're not anyone. You're potentially a Nobel, for God's sake. If the journals get out, if people know these are your real opinions –

Mallowan I used to twit Greene about that. I used to say, it's not the principle that's bothering you, Graham, is it? – it's the money. (*He gestures vaguely at a pile of shoeboxes.*) His letters are over there, somewhere – with all those from Updike and Golding and Beckett, and who's that Jap who committed hara-kiri, Mish-mash? –

Watkins Mishima? You have copies of your replies?

Mallowan Replies?

Watkins You don't write back?

Mallowan Once in a while. They're pestering buggers, some of them.

Counter-attacking, Mallowan catches Watkins off guard by pulling a sheet of paper from another precariously balanced pile.

Here. Look. Your first letter to me. Introducing yourself. It says here – in black and white – your foremost concern is the Work, the Life's only of importance in the light it throws on it –

Watkins You don't think your journal entries are relevant to a reading of the Work?

Mallowan (*slyly*) You said yourself, you could read every word of the novels and not have a clue.

Watkins That's because you concealed your real opinions.

Mallowan I didn't conceal them. I put them where they belong.

Watkins is struggling for air.

Watkins When Hector Gracechurch, for example, falls in love with Major Owolowe's daughter – what's your real opinion of that?

For the first time Mallowan looks heated.

Mallowan I started writing when I was an insurance clerk for the Co-op. I didn't ask to. It just happened. I get up in the morning, do my neccessaries, make myself a pot of tea and sit down there – (*Indicates his desk.*) – for the rest of the day. Making it all up. Out of my head. When I've done my pages for the day I potter around for a couple of hours, warm up whatever Mrs Harris has made for supper – not a meal, at her hands, that you would wish to linger over – read for a bit, spend a few minutes in the kazie – then to bed. Never see anyone, never do anything. (*Indicates the manuscript.*) I started writing about those buggers thirty-five years ago –

Watkins (*automatic*) Thirty-six –

Mallowan – and they've been round my bloody neck ever since. I've finally shut them up. I've given everything to them –

Don't you think, in the couple of hours a day I'm away from them, I'm free to have a life of my own? That I'm not entitled to *my* words, *my* opinions, instead of their interminable bloody rattle?

Watkins Rattle? Esterling's words of farewell to his son? Gracechurch's description of his mistress's body? *Rattle?*

Mallowan You want to try getting a word in edgeways.

Watkins Your words – the words in the journals – you do realize they make them unpublishable?

Mallowan is immediately alert.

Mallowan Unpublishable?

Watkins I think I hoped this was some gigantic mistake, some joke that you were playing. Or that they were an extended series of notes for a novel you'd yet to write, a caricature of provincial life –

Mallowan You can tell them from me, if the journals aren't publishable, I'll find someone else for the book and all.

Watkins You couldn't do that.

Mallowan Try me.

He pulls back, as if suddenly solicitous for Watkins, who looks as if he's about to hyperventilate.

In a bit of trouble, are you? Because you missed them?

Watkins (*weakly*) You could say that.

Mallowan Have a drop of this. (*He opens the lock on the sideboard, takes out an ancient bottle of sherry and a glass, locks the sideboard up again.*) Mrs Harris brought it a couple of Christmases ago. (*He uncorks it, sniffs it, wipes the glass with his thumb and pours.*) I won't have one myself.

Watkins sips the sherry, pulls a face, sips again as Mallowan watches, as if concerned about his well-being.

You look a little peaky.

Watkins I've been up for thirty-six hours. Flew in from California last night, two nights ago, whenever.

Mallowan Flew? That must be a terrifying experience.

Watkins Not really, no.

Mallowan They wanted to fly me to London once – (*He*

frowns, as if talking about some expedition to the furthest corners of the earth.) Some literary lunch or other. I thought about it. (*Even more he looks as if he's talking about a dangerous venture to the other side of the world.*) I weighed it up but no, not for me.

Watkins Larkin never went abroad either, did he?

Mallowan chuckles.

Mallowan He said somebody once told him, if he ever went to America, go to either the east or the west coast – the rest is a desert full of bigots.

Watkins You never wanted to travel? Lecture?

Mallowan (*to the new manuscript*) I've had those sods on my back –

Watkins Now they're out of your life?

Mallowan (*vaguely*) There's the garden, the roof needs fixing, there's always something to do.

Watkins You must get lonely.

Mallowan Not with buggers like you around. (*He pours another sherry for Watkins, looking around at the room.*) I must like it here, or I wouldn't be here, would I?

Watkins Like Proust in his cork-lined study. Writing away. Year after year.

Mallowan He didn't have you sticking your head in every twenty minutes.

Watkins sips the sherry, starting to get his balance back.

Watkins Is there anything – apart from the journals – that I might have missed?

Mallowan Which leg Uncle Alf lost.

Watkins Something important.

Mallowan It mattered to Uncle Alf. (*On impulse he unlocks the sideboard, takes out a second glass.*) Know what? – I don't mind if I do. (*He cleans the glass with his thumb, pours a small sherry for himself.*) It's not every day you finish thirty-five years of work, is it?

Watkins Thirty-six. (*He raises his glass.*) The Hotel Lucerne.

Mallowan Colonel Gracechurch.

Watkins Major Owolowe.

They chink glasses in a toast and Watkins sips his sherry, starting to relax.

Mallowan Something you might have missed? (*Thoughtful*) There's all that stuff about my brother –

Watkins chokes on the sherry, dabs at his shirt front.

Watkins Brother? You don't have – do you have a brother?

Mallowan I was an only child, it's true – (*Watching Watkins's distress with sly malice*) But – you're sure I didn't mention this? – I was a twin. Identical twin. I survived, my brother didn't. He was born with my umbilical cord around his neck. I'd strangled him. Manchester Royal Infirmary.

As Watkins struggles for words Mallowan pours another sherry for him.

Say when.

Watkins You – you strangled him?

Mallowan There weren't a lot of suspects, were there, in the circumstances. Even the Greater Manchester police could have sorted that one out.
 Are you sure I never mentioned it?

Watkins What – what effect did it have – have on you?

Mallowan You tell me. You're writing my life, I'm just trying to live the bugger. (*Malicious*) Maybe it slipped your mind.

Watkins grabs the sherry, fills his glass and swallows it in one.

Watkins Those images of blood and darkness in your work – Hans Esterling watching his brother choke to death, Lady Lydia's constant nightmares about the hands around her neck –

The banging, howling and barking start up, abruptly end.

Even this obsession with the roots coming into the house through the pipes –

Mallowan I never said?
There's always the second edition. There will be one?

Watkins This isn't – (*He swallows, tries to come to terms with the enormity of what he's just heard.*) This isn't second-edition stuff, I can't just slip it in – (*He pours another glass of sherry, knocks it back in one.*)

Mallowan Steady on. I was hoping to make that last.

Watkins I can't put this in a footnote or a preface – it clearly goes to the root of – (*Shaking his head, dazed*) – why you write. Why you bury yourself alive up here. Why you've never let anyone get close to you. In over three hundred pages I never refer to it once –

Mallowan Three hundred and sixteen. Including preface.

Watkins I'll never work again. Nobody will trust me with anything. I'll be a laughing stock.

Mallowan takes the bottle from his numb fingers.

Mallowan Do you mind? (*He unlocks the sideboard, puts the bottle away again, locks the sideboard.*) I expect you'll be wanting to get on.

Watkins This isn't something that slips your mind. You can't 'forget to mention' something like that.

Mallowan Well there again, maybe, wasn't it your job to ask the right questions? (*He flashes a pleasant smile.*) Did you have a hat? Coat?

Watkins Is there anything else? Anything at all? (*Refusing to leave, he confronts Mallowan.*) I'm not leaving until I know.

Mallowan That's the sherry talking.

Watkins I need to know how comprehensively my work, my career, my life have been shattered. Is there anything left of them whatsoever? (*Backing away.*)

Mallowan You'll be all right when you get in the fresh air.

Watkins Give me that list – (*He grabs it, flicks through it.*) Wolseley – Sundry Accounts – left leg – (*Turning it over*) Boring boring boring, detail detail detail – (*Reaching the end of it*) Is that it? That's all I missed or got wrong or had kept from me?

Mallowan (*irritated*) You're like some bugger who breaks into a chap's house. Asking the most personal, intimate questions. Keeps coming back, even when the chap thinks he's shot of him. Making notes. Following him around. Remembering everything about him. Even how long he's been in his house. Can't be got rid of, for love or money. Gets to know more about the chap than the chap knows about himself.

Watkins Except for the important, the crucial information.

Mallowan picks up Watkins's copy of the biography.

Mallowan *The Gloomy Englishman – A Life of Edward Mason Mallowan.*
A Life.
Not *the* Life. (*He finishes off his own sherry in one jerk of his head.*) I even let you have your head about Great-Uncle Bob.

Suddenly chilled, Watkins stares at him.

Watkins Don't – don't tell me you kept something from me about that –?

Mallowan (*careful*) It wasn't exactly keeping it from you –

Watkins What?

Mallowan It was more, well, letting you draw your own conclusion –

Watkins grabs his own and Mallowan's glass and drains them both.

Watkins My conclusion – my conclusion is a work of scholarship – of the most rig – (*swallows, tries again*) – rigorous scholarship. '*An academic detective story which immediately catapults Watkins into the foremost ranks of literary biographers.*' Saskatoon University Journal.
The tangled relationship between your father, Great Uncle Bob and your mother – Great-Uncle Bob's missing years –

Mallowan London. He was in London, it turns out. Not hiding from my dad, after all, like in your book. Where you take three chapters to prove it was him got me mum up the duff.

Watkins London?

Mallowan I was looking through some letters the other day – (*Indicates one of the shoeboxes.*) You're going to laugh – (*He pulls a letter out. Ignoring it*) It's all so much more ordinary and yet quite preposterous at the same time, like Great-Uncle Bob himself.

The family secret for all those years was his employment in Selfridge's.

It was Great-Uncle Bob's job to wait in the staff canteen in his celluloid collar until Lady So-and-So or Lord Such-and-Such made a complaint about an insufficiently servile assistant or tardy delivery. (*He shakes his head in amusement, chuckles.*) This'll kill you –

General Manager would express outrage and summons Great-Uncle Bob from the basement to his office, where he'd be dressed down and fired, handed his cards, there and then, on the spot.

Exit Great-Uncle Bob, head bowed, to return to the canteen to await his next dismissal. (*Shoulders shaking, he wipes his eyes with the handkerchief, puts the letter back in the envelope.*) Some families would have thought that was a hoot, but as far as mine was concerned, both sides regarded it as shameful, as if he'd been caught behind the altar sucking off the Methodist Superintendent.

Watkins sways, as if his legs won't support him. With a kind of delicate malice, Mallowan takes the sherry glasses from him.

D'you mind? They're worth a bob or two.

Watkins stares at him, mouth working but nothing coming out.

The interesting thing is – you won't mind me saying this, I know – it was your one piece of real writing in the whole bloody shoot.

As a rule – and I know you can take a bit of honest

criticism – you handle the English language like a blind man attacking a hedge but your prose was alive suddenly. That bit's the one time in three hundred and sixteen pages you actually put a few words together without embarrassing yourself – I can say that to you, writer to writer, without hurting your feelings, I know I can – (*He picks up the copy of the biography again. Reads*) '*The shadow of the chapel hung over everything; the stopped clocks on the staircase, the constant smell of damp walls, damp carpets, damp clothes drying on the hallstand hooks; the rare, furtive, shamed gropings in the dark that passed for joyless sex and commitment without love –*'

Dead wrong, of course, my family went at it like knives, bonking mad they were, even for Methodists.

You have – and you'll take this in the spirit it's meant – a genius for taking a very firm grasp of the wrong end of the stick. I wonder where it comes from.

Totally routed, Watkins can only stand, open-mouthed, staring at him.

At first I put it down – you won't take this the wrong way? – to your limitations as a writer, your total inability to write a sentence anybody would care to get – I can be candid? – to the end of.

Then I realized it had to be something more.

I don't suppose it's ever occurred to you – it wouldn't – there's something very much of the portrait painter and his subject in the relationship I've reluctantly had to endure with your good self the past few years –

Mallowan is completely in command now, able to place his darts anywhere he chooses in Watkins's numb but quivering flesh.

One should remember, however, that isn't altogether a one-way street.

While the subject is being observed, he is also – follow

me, if you can – observing. As the painter adds brush stroke after brush stroke to the canvas, the subject is adding detail after detail to his own portrait of the painter. The subject's gaze – can you see where I'm going? – is as cruel, intense, alive and merciless as the painter's should be. They're in one another's hands, as close as any two people could be.

Moving in for the kill, with Watkins helpless.

I wonder what it is that makes a man decide that biography is what he's meant for – how – and I know you'll take this in the spirit it's meant – how he copes with the awful second-rateness of it – the grubbing up of dates and facts, hoping that if he puts enough twos and twos together he'll come up with something as unfathomable as a life.

It's not just – I think you'll agree with me – the sheer cheek, the brass neck of it – it's more like a spiritual failure, some colossal gap in understanding, of appreciation of the complexity of existence.

There's jealousy too, of course – you won't dispute that, I know – envy and wounded pride and bafflement that his own powers should be so limited and another's so protean – and there's maybe even – can we go so far as to say this? – *hate*, for his subject, too – what else could keep him going year after year, totting up the two by twos in his little notebook – a kind of *sullen* hate, not even a manly hate, a sneak's hate – we could call it – couldn't we? – a *second-rate* hate.

Dare we suggest – I think we do – there's also a laziness at work here? – a bone-idleness that all that notebook scribbling and aeroplane travel from one side of the world to the other tries to mask – the essential laziness of a man who decides that the path is too steep, the peak too distant to be gained by his own efforts – who chooses biography as a means of ascent to heights unscalable by his own meagre talents – if we don't have it in us to dare to be great, after all – encumbering those who do with our unwanted presence is better than nowt?

Moving in for the coup de grâce *as Watkins stares mutely up at him.*

Why does such a man keep going? For the threadbare rewards of academic life? A puff piece from Saskatoon – a place of storied learning, no doubt, but a little – provincial, in the last analysis?

Isn't it because – I think it is – he knows of the vacuum at the very centre of his being – his total unimportance in the universe of letters to which he's drawn and in which he's failed to make his own, original mark?

Somewhere in the busy make-work of the world of facts he can forget, if only for a moment, his own failures and inadequacies – more – forget the horror that if there is to be any meaning to his career or life – the Life and Work as you'd choose to call it – any even temporary celebrity or half-hint of immortality must be sought outside himself.

The hammering starts up again and the dog howls as Watkins sits rigid. Mallowan sounds conversational again.

I really should be keeping an eye on O'Halloran. He's cheap but, between you and me, he's been known to cut corners.

He opens the door and the banging and howling stop. Watkins heads like an automaton to it.

You'll be reporting back to the Scotsman, will you? Brasher, is it? (*Confidential*) You can tell him whether he goes ahead with the journals or not – and I do have a contract – it's highly unlikely I'll be giving him the new book.

Watkins opens his mouth to say something. Closes it again. Mallowan waits until he's in the doorway before picking up the copy of the biography which Watkins brought.

(*With a pleasant smile*) I think you'll understand, in all the circumstances, why I won't be asking you to sign this – (*Brightly*) Biography? I wouldn't wipe my arse with it.

The banging, hammering and howling start again as the lights snap out and we end Act One.

Act Two

SCENE ONE

The courtyard of Jessica and Neil's Tuscan villa. Doors lead off to the living quarters; a hammock is slung between a wall and a small tree; loungers are scattered around on the sun-baked stone.

The gate to the outside opens. Carrying an overnight case and a bag of groceries, Neil enters as Jessica talks to the notario *offstage.*

He looks around him, blissful to be there.

Jessica (*in Italian*) The papers, Signor Cattaneo. Before we sign anything we need to see the papers.

There's the purr of a small car rapidly departing and then silence. Jessica enters, also carrying an overnight bag and groceries.

He says there's an outstanding tax bill for the use of the public road. Would I give him a cheque made out to him directly for it?

Damn. I forgot to ask about the water.

Neil is touching the warm stone. As if he'd like to press his cheek against it.

Neil God, I love this house. It'll be hard to let it go. (*He sets his groceries and luggage down.*) In the old days no problemo. I'd have found something at the BBC to tide me over when Richter fires me.

It used to be such a wonderful place. A job for life or at the least always a pal who could give you a helping hand for a month or two – find a wee corner for you.

True, the offices always looked and felt like the Lost Property Department of Bulgarian State Railways, but there were nooks and crannies you could hide in for years or shelter for a time when things got too hot or desperate in the real world.

If the measure of civilization is the number of useless people it can support – those not directly engaged in agriculture or industry and so on – the old BBC was filled with more useless people than can ever have been collected in one time or place.

Now?

Jessica Maybe you should have volunteered to speak to Mallowan directly?

Neil What would have been the point? You saw poor old Watkins after the old bugger finished with him. (*He opens the door to the main house and looks in, regretfully.*) Will you buy me out?

I sell my half, it gives me six, seven months to figure what to do.

Jessica It doesn't have to come to that.

Neil Can you suggest any alternative?

Jessica The journals would have come to light sooner or later. Mallowan would have been exposed for what he is.

Neil A great writer.

Jessica You can't be defending him.

Neil When I listen to Wagner am I defending his anti-Semitism? When I watch *On the Waterfront* am I siding with Elia Kazan in naming names to the House Un-American Activities Committee?

Jessica To some degree, yes.

Neil So alongside the listings in *Time Out* should be a rating of the writer and performer's political probity?

Jessica It's a personal call.

They slice tomatoes, split bread, open the wine; preparing a meal on the courtyard table.

Neil So if the firm gets its hands on Mallowan's next novel – something which Watkins was suspiciously vague about – you won't touch it with a bargepole?

She hesitates.

Could it be your objection isn't on moral grounds as much as on that of taste?

Jessica Your nose is part of your moral equipment.

Neil You do agree Mallowan's a genius?

Jessica I'm not so sure of it as you.

Neil You were before you knew about the journals.

Jessica One's opinions of writers change over time.

Neil Not from one day to the next.

Jessica How can you defend Mallowan knowing what's in the journals?

Neil If I find that I can?

Jessica But you can't.

Neil knocks his wine back.

Neil I'm going to lie down. How about it? A wee legover? I don't know why but I always feel randy after a ride on a plane.

She doesn't move. Hurt, he heads towards the door leading to the house.

Jessica We should talk about this.

Neil We should drop it.
  I love you to pieces, you know that, but there are some times when your voice has that 'There's a yak turd on the shag-pile carpet' tone to it. Like just then.
  At this particular moment the fact that you are engaging me in debate in an American accent is a double annoyance. I can't help it, there it is. You are other. You are foreign. That accent and those flawless teeth are making it worse. Making my teeth ache, in fact.

Jessica Are they teeth? I thought you were having something done about them.

Neil These are British teeth, the products of socialized dentistry. Crumbling and stained though they are, they are a little part of my country's heritage. Uncle Sam will never get his hands on them.
  Coming? I'll make it quick.

She doesn't move and he goes through the door with what dignity he can muster, closing it solidly behind him. Before Jessica can follow there's the sound of a car outside, pulling to a halt.
  As she goes to the gate Richter walks through it. He looks appreciatively around the courtyard.

Richter Sure beats the Hamptons – by about a thousand years. Those poplars, the hills, that little village over there – (*Indicating the gate, from outside which comes the impatient honking of a horn.*) Can you pay the guy? I jumped on a plane, didn't have time to change my money.

Jessica Pisa?

Richter Rome.

A startled Jessica heads out. Left alone, Richter nibbles

a piece of bread, opens the doors, peers in, closes them again. Jessica returns, puzzled by his arrival.

What's that little building at the side of the house?

Jessica The *lemonaia*. It's originally where they stored lemons through the winter.

Richter Neil?

Jessica In the house. Lying down.
Couldn't resist the chance to fire him in person?

Richter looks at the food and drink.

Richter Can I –?

She nods and he tears some of the bread off, nibbles an olive, pours himself wine, as she looks on.

I think you could say there have been developments. Yes, you could certainly say that. In regards our little problem with Mallowan.
No thanks to Watkins, of course. (*Looking at her closely, as if puzzled*) I can't believe he was ever your type.

Jessica Is that anything to do with you?

Richter I don't think he handled Mallowan well. Saw him at breakfast. Poured grapefruit juice into his granola. Didn't seem to notice.

Jessica I never believed he was the man for the job.
Just to clear the air, you may as well know the whole thing didn't last more than three months and all the time he was scared stiff the faculty would find out. It was soon apparent that all he had to trade on was his English accent, he wasn't much of a teacher or researcher or a lover either. (*Realizing something about him*) You don't have any luggage.

Richter Straight to the airport. Didn't even have time to grab a toothbrush.

Jessica You will take care of Neil for six months or so, won't you? A year? Severance? He needs time to find something.

He moves closer to her.

Richter Is he my problem? Is it yours?

Jessica You're not Richard the Third, you shouldn't be trying to woo me over the corpse of his career.

Richter What exactly does he have to offer? What do any of these Brits have to offer? I'm not talking about in the sheets, that's between you and him – and Watkins and that poor sap Sedgewick and whoever else you've bedded on your way up.
  What do you see in them? They walk and talk like fags; they've no idea of business and they're not sober half the time. My God, have you seen how they drink?

Jessica And they spend long lunches talking about books and ideas instead of business strategy and marketing and positioning.

Richter Exactly.

Jessica They'd rather, even Hazeldene, that little shit, pass on the word about a new author than a stock tip. Somehow they've managed to keep their sense of this as a vocation, a calling, rather than a trade.

Richter Which is why the firm hadn't turned a quarter's profit in fifteen years.

Jessica It isn't about the price earnings ratio –

He surprises her by suddenly grabbing her by the arm.

Richter You tell me what it's about then. You take the

time to tell me. Say ten days in Acabonic Bay. Sailing. Tennis. The pool. (*Holding her even more tightly*) Couple of years, when I've pulled things into shape here, I'm going back to New York. Anything else is a backwater, you know that.

Jessica London, Paris, Rome?

Richter An apartment in Manhattan, weekends on Long Island –

Jessica My career had always been independent of personal relationships.

Richter Watkins, Sedgewick, Neil?

Jessica (*brightly*) Mentors.

Richter I'll mentor the fuck out of you. What do you say?

Jessica Could you repeat that? Preferably from, say, fifteen feet or more away.

He keeps hold of her.

Richter I want to fuck your brains out. I want to push you against that wall and stick it in you.

Jessica Let me think about that. And how it chimes in with the firm's sexual harassment policy.

Richter I was in the Marine Corps. That's how we do things.

Jessica That explains Vietnam.
My hand.

The door to the house opens and Neil stops dead as he sees Richter holding Jessica.

Neil Ben?

Richter lets Jessica go.

Neil What are you doing here?

Jessica Developments.

Neil Why was he –? Was what –? (*Puzzled*) Should I hit him? Is that appropriate? (*Sees Jessica rub her sore wrist*) Are you all right?

Jessica He was just demonstrating an old Marine Corps hold.

Neil (*to Richter*) You sent us packing, told us that Hazeldene and you would be having another go at Mallowan yourselves.

Richter heads to the table, pours wine for all three of them. He seems uncharacteristically hesitant. Almost as if he's reluctant to get to the point of what he has to say.

Richter An hour or so after you headed out we left Watkins in the hotel and took a cab to that shithole little house Mallowan lived in.
 I've never been outside of London in the three months I've been here and I can't say I've been missing much, from what I could see.
 Mallowan had been having some work done on the house –

Neil I heard it.

Richter Drains, an immersion heater, whatever that is –

Jessica It's what they call a water heater, over here.

Richter A gas heater, too. Some typically crude piece of British plumbing, no doubt –

He hands them each a glass.

Jessica (*refusing*) No.

Neil (*refusing*) Certainly not.

Richter There was a small crowd in the street. A police car, an ambulance, a fire truck –

Neil We say engine –

Jessica Neil –

She nudges him, nods for Richter to continue.

Richter It was only when Hazeldene and I pushed through the crowd that we realized all the activity was centred on Mallowan's house. Broken windows, charred drapes, people coming and going, a stretcher –

Neil Stretcher?

Richter Mallowan had used the cheapest guy he could find to do the installation, an Irish guy whose van pulled up just as we got there. O-something. They arrested him right away – or took him off for questioning or whatever they do here.

Jessica Get back to the stretcher –

Richter Mallowan went to bed last night –

Jessica It's Mallowan? Mallowan on the stretcher?

Richter Didn't I say that?

Neil As a storyteller, Ben, you're hardly in the Simenon class –

Richter There was a faulty connection or some piece of pipe missing – that's what they want to talk to the contractor about, I guess. The gas built up all night, six in the morning the pilot light in the stove ignites it or something – bang.

Neil Bang?

Richter Blew the windows out, damn near took the roof off, the ceiling falls in on Mallowan, followed by the chimney.
   He's gone.
   The dog's fine.

Neil Dog?

Richter Not a mark on him. Miraculous escape. I guess he'd have been happy to know that. That his faithful pet walked away from it.

Jessica Gone? What do you mean, gone?

Neil Narrative drive, Ben. Clarity of exposition. Forget the minor characters. Concentrate on our protagonist. What kind of shape is Mallowan in?

Richter As good as you can be when you're dead.

A beat, then Jessica and Neil reach for the wine simultaneously. They chug it back, look at each other, then at Richter.

Neil Could you go through the last bit again?

Jessica With a little more emphasis?

Richter He's dead. Mallowan is dead.

Neil and Jessica look at each other again. Neil takes their empty glasses, goes to the table, pours, hands her a drink, drinks with her, looks at Richter again.

Neil Go back to taking the cab from the hotel –

Jessica Mallowan's dead, Neil. He's telling us that Mallowan is dead.

Neil Blown up by a gas heater? No. Mallowan? Mildly suffocated by fumes from a charcoal stove like Balzac, perhaps – yes, I could see that, but an explosion? Nothing in his life suggested he could go out like that.

Richter I made it up?

The phone rings inside.

Richter Don't answer it. We haven't figured a media strategy yet. I told Hazeldene not to speak to anybody, local, national or international.

Jessica He came here without a toothbrush.

Neil I don't give a shit. That's my phone.

Richter I left Hazeldene at the house. He'd be a lot less conspicuous than me.

Jessica Conspicuous?

Neil runs his hands through his hair, suddenly struck by the immediacy of it all.

Neil I spoke to Mallowan yesterday. Only yesterday I spoke to him. We were there, yesterday, a few miles from him.

Jessica is more interested in what Richter might be holding back.

Jessica Why should it matter? If you were conspicuous?

Neil (*oblivious*) That lonely old bastard. Nothing in his life but his work and making things difficult for other people. The poor sod.

He wanders indoors as a defensive Richter answers Jessica.

Richter I didn't get much out of Watkins after his visit of the previous afternoon but he did confirm that Mallowan had finished the last novel in *The Hotel Lucerne* sequence. Who knew if it was still intact? There could have been smoke damage, water damage. Even if it survived there could have been problems with the estate – if probate here is anything like it's back home, we could have been tied up for months or years – and with a property like this –

Jessica That's all you could think of? As they wheeled him past you? Getting your hands on his novel?

Richter What better time to protect his interests as well as ours than when the front door is wide open and people are rushing in and out?

Jessica You sent Hazeldene in to steal the manuscript?

Richter You can hardly steal your own property. We're Mallowan's publishers.

Jessica Did he get it?

Richter I don't know.

Jessica Perhaps that's him now –

She looks towards the house, conscious that the phone's stopped ringing.

Richter I told him – nothing on the phone.
It's called fiduciary responsibility. They may not teach it in Creative Writing –

Neil heads out, still a little stunned.

Neil The *Independent*. Morton Bosgrove. He'd like two pars for tomorrow's edition.

Richter What did you tell him?

Neil That we're still in shock. We'll get back to him.

The phone rings again but Richter shakes his head.

Jessica (*sarcastic*) What if it's Hazeldene? Wanting to be bailed for pinching the book.

Neil What's happened to Hazeldene?

Jessica Ben had him steal the manuscript.

Neil Nice work. Is it good?

Jessica's shocked at his reaction.

Jessica Neil –

Neil Isn't that the question to ask?

Jessica Mallowan's not been dead for –

Richter Fourteen hours.

Neil But we do have the manuscript?

Richter There's a contingency in place.

Neil Thank God.

Jessica How can you say that?

He sees she's really upset.

Neil Thank God he lived long enough to finish it.

Jessica The book? That's all you can think of?

Neil (*puzzled*) Twenty minutes ago Mallowan was beneath contempt. Now you expect what, exactly? For Ben just to leave it lying there? In the rubble? Out of sentiment?

Jessica How about taste?

Neil There you go again, confusing morality with aesthetics.

Jessica (*needling*) How soon are you going to be rushing the Memorial Edition out?

Richter We will of course be looking to see if we should be making arrangements to meet demand caused by this tragic event –

Neil It could be Elvis and Bob Marley all over again. Only more tasteful. And not quite as lucrative. (*Abashed*) In fact, not like it at all, really.

Jessica sits at the table. Speechless. Watching Neil and Richter pool their energies.

Richter I'd like you to start thinking of a memorial service. Somewhere big but class – St Paul's?

Neil Weddings only, I think.

Richter Westminster Abbey?

Neil I'll check.

Richter We'll get Watkins to write something, a couple of pages, mentioning his close relationship, personal distress, how excited he is that at least we have the last of the novels –

Neil Watkins is slow. A page a day man.

Jessica intervenes. Sardonic.

Jessica On the other hand he was with him the last afternoon. 'From our own correspondent, live from the deathbed.'

Neil We need something fast. Just to set the tone. *Universal acknowledgement as leading novelist of our day. Odds on for a Nobel.* Etc.

Richter You come up with something short and snappy. But dignified.

Neil Short, snappy, dignified and full of grief.

Richter Prominent references to the biography and the new book –

Neil I'll get on to it right away.

The phone, which has stopped ringing, starts up again.

Neil What do we do about that?

Richter Nothing. We keep the high ground. Control the flow of information. Make the plays from our playbook.

Jessica And span the watershed?

Ignoring her, Neil pushes a space clear on the table. Takes out a laptop computer from his overnight bag and opens it.

Neil
He disappeared in the dead of winter;
The brooks were frozen, the airports almost deserted
And snow disfigured the public statues;
The mercury sank in the mouth of the dying day.
What instruments we have agree
The day of his death was a dark cold day.

Richter It was in the low sixties yesterday.

Neil That was a poem by Auden. In memory of W. B. Yeats.

Richter Can we use it? It's out of copyright?

Neil I was getting myself in the mood – (*Types*) Giant of English literature – (*correction*) European literature – (*correction*) World literature – (*Looks up at Richter. Careful*) I shan't mention the journals, of course.

Jessica How long can you keep them quiet?

Neil Only we three and Hazeldene know about them –

Jessica And Alasdair.

Richter He publishes a word, I'll fire him.

Jessica He doesn't work for us. He's an academic.

Richter You know him better than any of us. What's his price?

She gives a cool smile.

Jessica I don't think that'll fly. He spent years getting nowhere until Neil gave him his life's work, Edward Mason Mallowan.

Neil stops typing, dismayed.

Neil It's true, Ben. He can make an entire career out of Mallowan. He's not going to allow himself to be elbowed aside now.

Does he still have the journals?

Richter (*reluctant to answer*) I guess.

Jessica (*cheerful*) Black mark there, Ben.

Richter (*defensive*) I left Manchester without even a toothbrush –

Neil Laying aside the oral hygiene motif for a moment, what about formally commissioning him to edit them? We'll get him to sign a confidentiality agreement, he's to say nothing to anybody about them. They'll be his little secret.

Richter And then he publishes –

Neil He's so slow he'd make Flaubert look as if he had Tourette's Syndrome. It could take him three, four years to edit them properly. Longer, because we'll be very demanding about his scholarship.

We'll want a footnote for every name Mallowan mentions in the journals. Even if it's just the window cleaner. Footnotes to the footnotes. Citations. Cross-references. Indexing could take a year. More if we want a really really thorough job.

Then it disappears into Legal for another year. By the

end of that time, who knows, the bottom might have fallen out of the Mallowan market anyway. It might be time for a revisionist look at him, time to commission LeFèvre to do his usual demolition job – nothing spurs sales like a bit of controversy.

You see where I'm going, Ben? Try to take the journals from Watkins, try to squash him, it could blow up in our faces –

If, on the other hand, we make them his, stick them in his baggy corduroy pocket, as it were, he's our man.

Richter Have him in the tent pissing out instead of outside pissing in? Rope a dope?

Neil Whatever you mean by that – yes. (*Beat.*) Of course that means we all have to stay on board with the firm. There can be no idle talk of dismissals or laying blame.

Richter You screwed up bad.

Neil This may be true. But I refer you to your tent metaphor. Unattached to the firm I'd have no reason not to unzip my fly and aim in the firm's direction, would I?

Richter I dare you.

Neil Who'd have more to lose? You or me?

Richter knows he's over a barrel. Grunts.

Richter Don't screw up again.

Delighted at having saved his bacon, Neil looks around the courtyard and sighs.

Neil I really do like it here.

The phone rings again. Again it's ignored. Neil starts to type again.

Dickens – Zola – Tolstoy – Joyce – Mallowan –

Jessica Are there two g's in wogs? And is darkies i-e-s, or y-s?

Neil (*reproving*) Unconstructive.

Jessica The academic world's more of a sieve for gossip than publishing. They don't have anything else to do with their time. Sooner or later it'll slip out in a journal or at a conference.

Even if we were morally right to keep the journals quiet, it's in practice impossible.

Neil (*needling*) We? I thought you wanted no part of anything to do with Mallowan?

Richter turns on her.

Richter What exactly is your position, Jessica? Let's go heads-up on that.

The phone starts to ring again. Avoiding an answer she gets up, heads towards the house.

Let it ring.

Jessica I asked the *notario* to find a stonemason for the terrace. That might be him.

She heads inside, leaving Neil and Richter uncomfortably together. Richter's still looking at the door she's slammed behind her.

Richter Tough broad.

Neil Is that meant as a compliment?

Richter (*surprised*) What else could it be?

Neil (*sigh of incomprehension*) The Atlantic seems to me wider and wider every year.

Richter She'll go with the programme? Keep quiet about the journals?

Neil Unless we make the whole thing a matter of principle for her.

Richter I thought she made her way up on her back – (*Beat.*) Nothing personal.

Neil Taken in the spirit in which it was meant. (*He follows Richter's look at the door.*) On her back, knees, elbows, whatever. But just because of that we shouldn't assume she has no real passion for the Word.

Richter Can we trust her?

Neil On the way over I tried arguing with her about Mallowan's prejudices. Read her some words of G. K. Chesterton.

Somewhere he says something like *'The world is not a lodging house at Brighton, which we are to leave because it is miserable.*

'If we are confronted with a desperate thing – Pimlico, for example – it would not be enough to disapprove of Pimlico; in that case you'd merely cut your throat and move to Chelsea. Nor, certainly, is it enough for you to approve of Pimlico; for then it will remain Pimlico, which would be awful.

'The only way out would be for you to love Pimlico with a transcendental tie and without any earthly reason.

'In my search for a religious meaning to the world I found this hole in it; the fact that one must somehow find a way of loving the world without trusting it.'

There were tears in her eyes when I finished. She wept. And then I read her something else of Chesterton's –
I knew a Doctor Gluck
And his nose it had a hook
And his attitudes were anything but Aryan;
So I gave him all the pork
That I had, upon a fork
Because I am myself a vegetarian.

Richter What did she make of that?

Neil What do you think?
You Yanks like moral certainty. We're not rattled by shades of grey.

Richter pours himself the last of the bottle of wine, takes a paperback book out of his pocket.

Richter I've been reading him. Mallowan.

Neil One more sale. It all adds up.

Richter No. *Reading* him. Can't put the sonofabitch down. Take it to the john. Read it to three, four in the morning. The characters, the moral dilemmas – can't get them out of my head. And then I remember the journals.

Neil Wittgenstein said if a man tells you that two and two equals five, there's a problem but you can still communicate. If he says they equal ninety-seven, forget it.
I say we concentrate on the practicalities –

At that moment there's the sound of a car labouring towards the villa. They look at each other.

Richter The *Independent*?

Neil They wouldn't send someone all this way. Mallowan wasn't a rock star. (*He heads to the gate, opens it, looks out.*) Bloody hell –

The door to the living room opens and Jessica comes out.

Jessica It's Hazeldene.

Richter The phone?

Jessica The *Guardian*.
I didn't give anything away. Told them we'd have something in an hour or so.

Inside the house the phone rings again.

Damn.

They ignore it and watch the open gate, through which, in a moment, Hazeldene appears. He's carrying a large cardboard box, has no other luggage. He pats his pockets.

Hazeldene I seem to have –

Neil I'll get it.

Neil heads out, as Hazeldene peers around at the courtyard and buildings.

Hazeldene Fifteenth century?

Jessica With parts going back to the twelfth.

Hazeldene That's a *lemonaia* at the side of the house, isn't it?

Jessica Yes.

Neil comes back in from paying the cab driver. Looks closely at Hazeldene, who's dishevelled and not quite in possession of himself.

Neil Are you all right?

Hazeldene sees the wine on the table.

Hazeldene Mind if I –? (*He pours himself a very large drink, right to the top of the glass.*)

Richter What the hell are you doing here? (*He goes to the gate, looks out.*) Were you followed?

Hazeldene (*vague*) I'll be fine in a moment. (*He goes to drink, but the glass is still two inches from his mouth and spills all down his shirt front. He doesn't seem to notice.*)

Richter Did you get the book?

Hazeldene indicates the cardboard box, nods.

Hazeldene In there. With a couple of other little odds and ends.

Neil The journals?

Hazeldene Ah – there you are, Neil. Yes. (*Nods to Jessica*) Jessica – (*He sees the food.*) Could I –?
 Took the first plane here. Charter. One seat left. With the stuff in my lap all the way.

The phone starts to ring again.

Shouldn't someone get that?

Richter It'll keep. Anybody see you get the book?

Hazeldene starts to slice a piece of sausage.

Hazeldene There was so much confusion, people rushing in and out, the police and emergency services enjoying themselves tremendously. Took a quick shufty around, grabbed what I could – (*He keeps slicing, as if oblivious of what he's doing.*) Had to keep my wits about me, of course. If anyone asked me what I was up to I was going to tell them I was a relative. The arrival of a woman called Harris – some kind of charlady, I think, helped. Went into hysterics about a dog.

Neil Never knew Mallowan had one.

Hazeldene The world's full of surprises, isn't it? (*He is still slicing, as the sausage gets smaller and smaller.*) It's all in there – (*Indicates the box*) Manuscript, odds and ends, some of his foul papers – rough notes, first drafts, things like that –
 Stuffed them under my coat, Bob's your uncle and away we go – (*He stares at what's left of the sausage, shrugs, and starts to tug the bread apart.*) As the cab got nearer the hotel – where I intended to grab my things, say a fond farewell to Watkins and scarper, there were more police

cars, an ambulance or two, people milling around on the pavement. (*He keeps tugging at the bread. To Richter*) Uncannily like the scene at Mallowan's house, you'll remember. (*Momentarily forgetting the bread, he turns to Jessica.*) You were pretty close to Watkins at one time, weren't you?

Neil Were you?

Jessica He taught a course at Yale while I was there. That was all.

Before Neil can ask any more, Richter snaps an impatient question at Hazeldene.

Richter The journals. You did get them?

Hazeldene Oh yes.

Richter Watkins didn't put up a fight to keep them?

Hazeldene All the stuffing had been knocked out of him by that time.

Neil Yes, he was pretty shaken up by whatever happened between himself and the old bastard. (*Beat.*) The late old bastard.

Hazeldene turns back to the bread and keeps tearing pieces off it without eating.

Hazeldene He was, yes. In shock, almost.
After you and I left him, Ben, to go to Mallowan's house he had lunch in his room – an egg-white omelette, fruit salad, decaf – then he was seen in the lobby talking to himself.
The concierge asked him if he was all right and he said he'd be fine after a walk.
He stepped out of the hotel and – it must be presumed – forgot that he was no longer in California and that traffic moves on the left-hand side of the street – and was

mown down by a corporation bus. Number 23.

He died in the ambulance on the way to the hospital. (*He finishes tearing the bread apart.*) Any cheese?

Richter He's dead?

Jessica Alasdair's dead?

Hazeldene I told you. Had the stuffing knocked out of him. Literally.

There's a pause, then Neil abruptly bursts into peals of laughter. Richter and Jessica watch, appalled, as he throws his head back, consumed with mirth. Eventually he gets control back, puts on a serious face.

Neil I'm sorry. It's so ridiculous. (*He snorts with laughter and takes a moment to compose himself again.*)

Jessica You're sure he's dead?

Hazeldene has found the cheese and is stuffing it into his mouth, as if not even aware of what he's doing.

Hazeldene Went to the hospital. Found the ambulanceman. Spoke to him. No question about it. Watkins was babbling about an Uncle Bob all the way there, then shut up and that was it. (*Still stuffing cheese in his mouth.*) Back to the hotel, a quick rummage through his room, throw the journals in there – (*Indicating the box*) and here I am. Not entirely sure of how I got here, matter of fact. (*Cheese stuffed in his mouth, he stares around, as if seeing them for the first time.*) Neil – Jessica – Ben – (*A huge yawn.*) It's been a long day. Mind if I lie down?

Neil Go ahead –

He indicates the door to the living area but Hazeldene falls to the floor and stretches himself out prone at their feet.
    Even Richter is taking some time to take it all in.

Richter Shit. Holy steaming shit.

Neil What are the odds? I mean – what are the odds?

Jessica looks at him with a stiff face, tears almost about to flow.

Jessica You laughed. You laughed.

Neil Nervous reaction. More a giggle.

She reaches across and slaps his face.

Better now?

Jessica None of us cared. None of us bothered enough.

Neil We all did have our own problems and he was, after all, responsible for the entire mess, wasn't he?

Jessica He deserved to get run over?

Neil (*protesting*) I liked Alasdair. I gave him the damned biography, didn't I? In the teeth of your opposition. I was planning on letting him edit the journals.

The phone rings and an upset Jessica heads into the house.
Neil pulls the laptop towards him.

What's the right thing in these circumstances? A joint obit? United in death as in life – Too sentimental? (*Looking down at Hazeldene*) When exactly did Watkins kick the bucket?

Hazeldene responds, from the floor.

Hazeldene As they pulled into the hospital.

Neil The Royal?

Hazeldene Yes.

Neil Where Mallowan was born almost exactly sixty-four years ago. (*He suddenly shivers.*) That's great. Christ, that's great. If I can't do something with that – (*He turns wondering back to the laptop.*) Both of them. Just like that. Bingo. What are the chances?

As he types, Richter turns to Jessica, who's coming back out of the house.

Jessica Austin Moberly. Channel Four. They want to send a film crew over.

Richter We'd better check it's really in there. (*He takes out a manuscript from the box. To Hazeldene*) Is this it?

Hazeldene squints up from the floor.

Hazeldene Yes.

Richter takes the journals out.

Richter And all seven of the journals?

Hazeldene '67 to '99.

Neil stops typing.

Neil Whatever happened between the two of them – and we'll never know for sure now – could it have been – is there any possibility that Watkins bumped him off?

Richter Blew the house up? Then killed himself?

Jessica (*warning*) Neil –

The phone rings again.

Richter (*sceptical*) A little elaborate, wouldn't you say? An explosion? Why not just bang him over the head?

Neil P. G. Wodehouse has a very funny essay somewhere about the villains in fiction who bring about their own comeuppance though what he calls 'a fatal excess of ingenuity'. Lowering tarantulas on long threads over their intended victim's bed and so on.

Jessica This isn't fiction.

Neil I can see a book in it. Maybe two or three. In time it could be the Kennedy assassination conspiracy theory of the literary world. They're still arguing over who killed Marlowe.

Excited at the prospect, he resumes typing as Richter pulls out a shoebox from the cardboard box.

Richter Are these the odds and ends?

Hazeldene squints up again.

Hazeldene Letters to Mallowan from other writers.

Jessica Letters? (*As if pulled by a magnet, she heads towards the shoebox, pulls a handful of letters out.*) Malraux – (*another*) Neruda – (*This time she picks up a very small postcard with one word on it.*) Beckett – (*reaching for another letter*) Norman Mailer wants to fight him – (*another*) Greene wants his help with a plot –

She reaches for another but her hands are trembling.

My God. I mean – my God.

It's like some secret spider web of writers and reputations with Mallowan at its centre – (*She quickly riffs through more of them.*) Asking him for advice – thanking him for suggestions – '*Thank you for the idea of a novel about Islam. It's risky but I'll try it. Could be fun. Salman Rushdie. P S I love the title you suggest, too.*'

Richter indicates the letters now scattered on the table.

Richter Is there a book in there?

Jessica A book? This is going to mean revising the whole critical canon. Reputations are going to have to be re-evaluated from the ground up. It's a revolution.

Hazeldene She's right. We always knew Mallowan was important but even a quick butcher's at those –

Jessica (*to Hazeldene*) Were there more?

Hazeldene At least another three shoeboxes. Crammed full. Sometimes he hadn't even opened the envelopes.

Jessica This is the Fat Man and Little Boy of twentieth-century fiction. Nothing is ever going to be the same after this. Entire university departments are going to be wiped out.

Richter's keen nose for trouble starts to twitch.

Richter He wrote back? There might be letters out there with the same crap that's in the journals?

Jessica's numb fingers continue to pick up the letters and sift through them.

Jessica From the tone of these I don't think so. They're all embarrassingly fulsome.
   A journal is different from a letter, anyway. The confessional impulse is separate from the epistolary.

Hazeldene (*plaintive*) I do think I might be given some credit for getting our hands on all this – the journals, especially. It's not an easy thing to rifle a dead man's possessions.

Richter You did great. (*Beat.*) We still have the problem with the journals, though.

Neil looks up again.

Neil Do we?

The phone rings again, ignored.

Mallowan's death – deeply regretted though it is – the rescue of his last book and the discovery of the letters make him all the more valuable a property. Even the coincidence of Alasdair Watkins checking out at the same time – for whatever reason – can only add to the legend.

The biography isn't a problem. We can let it die a natural death. Poor old Alasdair isn't here to press for a second edition. (*He picks up the journals.*) We turn to these. They are here. We four are here. We four who are the only ones who know about them.

But say by some mischance they never saw the light of day, the knowledge of their existence never went beyond the four of us? Say five minutes after Hazeldene arrived they'd been buried in a mudslide or an earthquake. Would the world be a poorer place?

Say, even more interestingly, a small fire had broken out –

Richter How small?

Neil Small. But intense. About six inches by four.

Say – and do tell me if I'm losing anyone here – say tomorrow morning or better, this evening, or better still, right away, they were to find themselves on the leaf pile out there beside the *lemonaia* and by some mischance someone were to drop a match on it and it not be noticed until it was too late – well, then, it would be too late, wouldn't it?

Silence as his words are digested.

I'll go through it again, shall I? Diaries, fire, ashes, *no problemos*.

Jessica Prison?

Hazeldene gets back on his feet. He's still shaky but starting to recover.

Hazeldene If this idea of Neil's – *Neil's* – *w*ere to be carried out, I'm not entirely sure what offence would have been committed. Whose property are the journals? They were given to Watkins.

Jessica Then stolen from him.

Hazeldene Rescued. Like the manuscript. And the letters.

Neil What's their intrinsic value? A set of battered old notebooks? Five, six pounds? If that.

Jessica It's not their worth as objects, it's what's inside them.

Neil Racist abuse. Ugly words. Prejudice.

Richter sees a problem.

Richter The cat's out of the bag already. We made an announcement.

Hazeldene pours himself another drink. This time he manages to drink it properly.

Hazeldene Correct me if I'm wrong, but didn't we say only we had reached an agreement with Mallowan to publish them? – That's a very far cry from saying we had possession of them.

Neil Perhaps they disappeared in the explosion. Or afterwards. A terrible loss to literature, of course.

Hazeldene They might become objects of literary myth – the Mallowan Diaries – where are they? – what did they contain?

Neil (*to Jessica*) You may be seized with a desire to expose Mallowan for what he was but the inevitable price of that is Alasdair's reputation. Collateral damage, I think they call it.

Hazeldene's getting back to his old, sharp form.

Hazeldene We don't really know what passed between

Watkins and Mallowan yesterday afternoon, before one of them was assassinated by the Gas Board and the other by the Transport Department – but might it not have been that at some point in their colloquy Mallowan asked Watkins to make sure his reputation remained intact by destroying his journals?

Jessica There's nothing to say that happened.

Neil There's nothing to say it didn't.
  He may have told Watkins that the journals were just a joke, as we all suspected, he was having fun with them, they were never really meant to see the light of day –

Jessica He signed a contract to publish them.

Neil All part of the joke. He told Watkins that he always intended backing out. Again, there's nothing to say it didn't happen that way.

Hazeldene Wouldn't that fit in with the Mallowan we knew?

Jessica We didn't know him. Nobody knew him. The work, yes, the books, but not him.

Hazeldene (*triumphant*) There you are then. We didn't know him one way or the other so there's nothing we can rule out. It's entirely possible that his dying wish was for us to torch them.

The phone rings again and Neil moves close to Jessica.

Neil In a very few minutes somebody will have to talk to them. Do we want to have poor old Alasdair pilloried in his grave because he'd overlooked maybe a couple of thousand words in the hundreds of thousands that Mallowan wrote?

Hazeldene looks towards the house.

Hazeldene I presume you use candles? There would be a box or two of matches lying around somewhere?

Neil Next to the sink. Second shelf.

Hazeldene heads inside the house, past Richter, who's not taking part in any of this.

What would be lost, after all? Aside from the racist bilge, which you despise anyway? Mallowan's opinions on the price of things, his recording of his bowel movements, observations on day-to-day life in a not particularly interesting small town on the edge of nowhere?

Jessica It's the racist bilge that's the point –

Neil So you'd publish it? Destroy his reputation?
Weigh it against the value of his other writing and ask yourself which you'd rather lose – those grubby notebooks or *The Hotel Lucerne* – and all those other novels in which real human beings struggle with the eternal moral issues.
Are there so many writers obsessed with those issues that we can afford to have Mallowan taken off the shelves? Discredited? Remaindered for good?
You're entitled to your opinion about who he was in his private life – (*Puts one of the journals in Jessica's hands*) But if you really mean what you say about the evil in there – you'll help me make a bonfire of it.

As Jessica hesitates, Hazeldene comes out of the house with a box of matches in his hand. He's holding one match up as if he'd never seen it before.

Hazeldene What a wonderfully simple piece of design the match is. You can't go wrong with one. Even a child could use it. (*Rattles it*) And how many you get in a box.

He tosses the box to Neil, who catches it. Hazeldene heads towards the gate.

I'll be off, then. Don't bother to call a cab. The walk will do me good.

Neil darts between Hazeldene and the gate, stopping him leaving.

Neil We're all in this together.

Richter breaks his silence.

Richter Give them to me.

With alacrity Neil tosses the box to him.

Neil That's the spirit.
That's where you have to hand it to the suits. When it comes to action they've got us literary types beat hands down.

Richter The journals. All of them.

Cheerfully Neil hands them to him.

Neil I'd recommend burning them page by page. (*He starts to rip sample pages out.*) It'll take longer but what's the hurry? (*He opens the gate.*) You can't miss it. By that wee shed at the side.

Richter Get me a cab.

Neil nods to Jessica.

Neil Tell them it'll be an hour. Make it two. Some of those notebooks are pretty thick.

Richter I'm going back to London. I'm taking the journals.

Hazeldene You're the boss, Ben, but getting rid of them here and now is much, much safer.

Richter (*to Jessica*) You're right. We have no right to do this.

Neil thinks he understands, grins.

Neil Nice one, Ben. (*To Hazeldene*) Relax. He'll incinerate the buggers in private. (*An admiring shake of the head*) You bean-counters –

Richter We're not going to publish but we're not going to destroy them.

Neil We get it, Ben, we get it, okay? You're covering your arse.

Jessica He means it. (*To Richter*) Don't you?

Richter nods.

Neil Then give me the bloody things.

Richter They're the property of the firm.

Neil Bollocks. Hazeldene stole them.

Richter On my behalf.

Neil You told him to steal the book. The journals were a little foreigner on his own account – (*Appealing to Hazeldene*) Right?

Hazeldene is nervous, not wanting to alienate Richter.

Hazeldene If Ben thinks it's too risky –

Richter Not risky. Wrong.

Neil Oh please, don't give me that. (*Heading towards Richter*) Hand them over.

Richter squares up.

Richter I was a Marine. I'm combat qualified.

Neil I used to work for the BBC Arts Department. I saw action too. (*All the same, he backs off.*) Jessica, tell him, for Christ's sake, this is no time to be bandying about words he doesn't understand.

Jessica This is for real, Ben, isn't it?

Richter There's a principle.

Neil Principles are our business. Profits are yours.

Richter They're his words.

Hazeldene (*cautious*) Words like darkies and nigger –

Neil And Yid. And kike. And heebs.

Richter I don't *like* the words –

Jessica We have a First Amendment tradition. It guarantees everyone the right to say what he wishes and everyone else the right to hate it.

Neil Isn't there also some right to privacy? All Hazeldene and I are suggesting is that poor old misguided Mallowan be allowed that.

Hazeldene (*skittish*) Now hang on, Neil –

Neil You're suffering, Ben, from the almost superstitious sense of reverence the man of business has for the written word. Abstract arguments over principle should be kept where they belong – between the covers of a book – and not allowed to confuse our actions in the real world.

The phone starts ringing again.

Mallowan, in his private life, is revealed as a monster. He hates everybody for the most banal yet dangerous of reasons – they're different from him.

In his life in literature Mallowan is something else entirely.

I don't pretend to understand the dichotomy but I care passionately that his public voice be preserved.

Richter I'm not defending his opinions but his right to express them.

Neil You wouldn't have burned *Mein Kampf* if Hitler offered it to you in 1925?

Richter That's ridiculous.

Neil Somebody published it. At some point they must have had the manuscript in their hands.

Richter It wasn't me.

Neil In the Kingdom of Letters debate proceeds by speculation, hypothesis, metaphor. You want to muscle in, you have to play by our rules.

Richter I wouldn't have published it.

Neil But would you have destroyed it? If you had, say, the single copy in your hands?

Richter (*playing for time*) *Mein Kampf*?

Neil By A. Hitler. A promising young author.

Richter The only copy?

Neil Fedexed to you.

Richter In 1925?

Neil In Munich.

Jessica This isn't fair.

Neil I'm just trying to help him out.
  Let's say that Himmler had written poetry –

Jessica Himmler?

Neil Not as far-fetched as all that. Goebbels was a published novelist.
  Say that one day some of Himmler's poetry turned up and it wasn't all that bad. It wasn't Goethe but he was a surprisingly gifted minor lyrical poet –

Richter Couldn't happen.

Neil Say it did –

Richter (*stubborn*) It didn't.

Neil Say there are six or seven pages of publishable material – love poems, nature poems. Don't you think whoever had the opportunity to publish them should think long and hard about their responsibility?
  Suddenly Himmler and the rest of the squalid gang of thugs aren't quite that, are they?

Hazeldene weighs cautiously in.

Hazeldene Not that I'm taking sides, but say we publish and a reader who worships Mallowan reads the journals, too. At first he dismisses the racist nonsense for what it is – then he begins to have second thoughts. If his hero Mallowan can believe this, is there something in it?

Neil The word changes the world. What was in Pandora's box but the gift and the curse of language?

Jessica Stick to your principles, Ben. Take the journals and go. I may even come with you.

Neil has shot his bolt for now. Appeals to Hazeldene.

Neil Hazeldene –

Hazeldene Here's my two penn'orth, for what it's worth –
  I respect your opinion, Ben, and yours, too, Jessica, but it seems to me we're all a little out of our depth here. We're publishers, we're used to dealing with the *printed* word. The principles and scruples we bring to bear on that may not be the same we need now.

Jessica So we can censor the journals simply because they're in his handwriting?

Hazeldene We didn't stop him saying what he thought,

did we? That would have been censorship. After the event, after the word is spoken, we could call it, well, *editing*.

Dramatic, even drastic editing, I agree, but well within the privileges of the genre –

Jessica Editing by blowtorch?

Hazeldene If it's the *morality* of the thing –

I'd say there's no question what's the moral position to take given a choice between an abstract principle that protects the dissemination of hate and the concrete good of the avoidance of harm.

Neil's got his second wind.

Neil Bugger morality. It's a question of expediency. Morality always answers to some abstract ideal, expediency is to do with real people in the real world; it's the higher imperative. (*He goes to the gate, indicates the vista beyond.*) See that line of poplars there? On the hill line? It goes all the way to the next village. Pretty damn picturesque, eh? After the war they planted one for every partisan or hostage who died. Not just men – women and children, too. I've never counted them but you're in shade all the way. (*To Richter*) What about it, Ben? Six million dead in the camps, twenty million dead all over the world, because somebody's middle-class scruples stopped him from taking action when it could have done some good. (*He holds his arms out for the journals.*) I'll wait until you're gone, if you like. (*A quick look at Jessica*) You too.

Richter hesitates, then throws the journals on the table, one by one.

Matches?

Richter takes them out of his pocket, hesitates again, then makes his mind up.

Richter Beans need counting. Somebody get me a cab.

Neil Jessica?

She's staring at Richter.

Jessica God, you were so *beautiful* there for a moment.

Neil You can leave it with us. We know what we're doing. (*to Hazeldene*) The number of the firm we use is beside the phone.

Hazeldene heads to the door as Richter tosses the box of matches at Neil. It never arrives. Jessica grabs it mid-flight.

Jessica No.

Hazeldene stops dead.

I can't let you burn a book, even a notebook, even a book with such vile things in it. You can call it the triumph of taste over judgement but it's not an image I'm comfortable with, it's not something I'm going to be party to.

Neil I thought you were leaving with Ben?

Jessica I'll still be complicit.

Richter's had enough.

Richter Forget it. You want to share a cab? Let the sonofabitch do what he wants.

Jessica You can't walk away from this.

Richter The damn things are stolen. You hate everything in them. Where's your problem?

Jessica I thought it was your problem too, a moment ago –

Richter Give me a balance sheet, a column of figures, the quarterly earnings – they tell you all you want to know, no bullshit, no confusion, there's a truth to them – (*Stabs a finger at Hazeldene*) His crap – (*And at Neil*) And his crap – (*At her*) Even your crap, it makes my head hurt, it goes round and round, you think you're getting somewhere, you see an answer, a *position*, some other fucker jumps in with something else and you see it all different –

Jessica My crap?

Richter I want something I can hold on to. Something that tells me something factual. Numbers do that. Words shift around too much.

Jessica You'd let him burn a book?

Richter He could torch the New York Public Library is what I feel right now, as long as I get that cab.

Hazeldene Coming right up. (*He skitters into the house.*)

Richter Know something else? (*He takes the paperback copy of* Notes from Hut Seven *out of his pocket.*)

Richter You can add this to it.

He throws it towards Neil.

Richter The *Financial Times*, the *Wall Street Journal*, my stock analysis spreadsheets – that's what I'm reading from now on. (*To Jessica*) My stuff, you look at the numbers the end of the business day, you know where you are. Your stuff, somebody's got a bigger mouth, a faster lip, *opinions*, you end up not even knowing what you think. (*Scornfully*) Fiction? I don't believe a word of it.

Hazeldene sticks his head around the door.

Hazeldene What's the Italian for taxi?

Neil Taxi.
Is there another box of matches in there?

Hazeldene disappears again as Jessica grabs the journals, hugs them to her.

Jessica I won't let you burn even one book in my name.

Neil Even though you hate every word in those ones?

Jessica Yes.

Neil Your position is ludicrous, can't you see that?

Jessica It being ludicrous is no test of its tenability. Read your Mallowan. His characters are constantly up against the paradoxes of the moral universe.

A flustered Hazeldene sticks his head around the door again.

Hazeldene Can't seem to find them –

Neil (*to Jessica*) Give me the bloody journals.

Jessica No.

Hazeldene Point made, Jessica, now put a sock in it –

Jessica The hell with you. (*To Richter*) And you. (*To Neil*) How *could* you?

Neil ignores her, turns to Hazeldene.

Neil Try the small glazed bowl on top of the fireplace.

Jessica You couldn't do it if it came down to it.

Neil No?

Jessica You're still a romantic about this business.

Neil That's slander.

Jessica That's what I love so much about you.

Richter My cab?

Jessica I see the look on your face when you open a new

manuscript. The way you stick your nose into something just off the press.

Richter I don't give a good goddamn if he rubs his crotch against the bookshelves when he thinks nobody's looking – my cab?

Hazeldene shouts in triumph from inside the house.

Hazeldene (*offstage*) Got them! (*He rushes back on again, holding another box.*) The other wonderful thing about matches is they make them by the millions.

Neil catches them as Hazeldene tosses to them. Neil goes to the table and indicates the shoebox filled with letters.

Neil How many more of these are there?

Hazeldene Two at least. Maybe more.

Neil How hard would it be to get hold of them?

Hazeldene I imagine for a day or two people will be coming and going to what remains of the house.

Neil turns to Jessica again.

Neil One of the great themes in Mallowan's fiction is the impossibility of holding to any absolute moral standard. Time and again he poses such questions as, for example, what would be the greater evil – to lose these letters or the journals?

Jessica watches aghast as he strikes a match.

Jessica You wouldn't dare.

Neil To incinerate either would be wrong, of course, but we're sometimes presented with hard choices. (*He takes out a letter at random.*) John Updike.

Jessica No –

Neil calmly holds the match to the letter and watches it burn. Hampered by the journals, Jessica can only make a vague grab at the box, which Neil deftly hands to Hazeldene.

Neil (*to Jessica*) Let me burn the journals and you share only an indirect responsibility for their destruction. It's an entirely different case with the letters. (*He strikes another match. To Hazeldene*) Who's next? Beckett? Calvino? Tom Wolfe?

Jessica You're a madman.

Neil Possibly. But I hold the matches. That's always made a difference.

Jessica appeals to Richter.

Jessica You can't let this happen –

Richter (*to Hazeldene*) Is that cab on its way?

Jessica You can't stand by and let him do this.

Richter When we took over Peabody and Schaumburg I fired twenty guys in one morning. Every one of them broke down and cried. I slept like a baby.

Hazeldene hands Neil another letter.

Hazeldene José Saramago – (*To Richter*) Nobel Prize for Literature, 1998.

Neil brings the match close to the letter.

Neil What we really need, of course, is an editor for these letters whose ambition matches the potential of them. Someone who won't be intimidated by the prospect of excavating the greatest literary treasure trove of our times.

You put it very well, Jessica. It's a revolution. It'll make the career of whoever's lucky enough to get it. A lifetime of blowing up reputations and having the last word. Polemics, controversy and mayhem in academe. They'll win every literary fist fight they get into because they'll have the goods on everybody, like the Godfather. (*To Richter*) I wonder, Ben, where we'd find someone who could measure up to the job?

Richter Jessica? What do you say?

Jessica If the price is the journals –

Richter You're right. It is.

Neil It's not every day that the moral imperative fits in so well with naked self-interest. I should make the most of it.

A beat, then Jessica puts the journals back on the table. Neil instantly gathers them up in his arms.

Neil Hazeldene –

At a nod from Neil, Hazeldene hands her the shoeboxes as there's the distant honking of a small car, getting nearer.

(*To Hazeldene*) You'll be going back with Ben. Don't get greedy, just the shoeboxes. We want you for literature, not a life of crime.

Hazeldene heads to the table, picks up the manuscript.

(*Sharply*) No you don't. You can leave that here.

Hazeldene I don't think so.

Richter looks from one to the other.
Hazeldene has a tight hold of the manuscript, as Jessica grasps the shoebox of letters and Neil the journals.
Richter barks a harsh, contemptuous laugh.

Richter The world of books.

He heads out. Hazeldene follows, hugging the manuscript to his chest.

Hazeldene Strange how Italy is filled with people you see all the time back home.

He exits. After a moment there's a slamming of car doors, the sound of the cab retreating and all is silence again.
   Neil and Jessica have been staring at each other all this time, holding their respective prizes.
   Neil heads out.
   Jessica goes to the table, spills out the letters. She stares at them, as if she can't quite believe it.
   She starts to sort through them as smoke begins to drift in from outside. A beat, then Neil reappears. She doesn't look up.

Neil Who have you got there?

Jessica Gabriel Garcia Marquez. (*Beat.*) You made that up about the poplars, didn't you?

Neil Yes.

She takes her reading glasses from her case and sits. In a moment she's engrossed in the letters. Neil sits the other side of the table from her, at his laptop.
   He scratches his chin, seeking inspiration.

Dickens – Zola – Tolstoy – Joyce – Mallowan – Boswell – Carlyle – Strachey – Holroyd – Watkins –

He starts to type as the smoke gets thicker and thicker. The lights start to fade as we –
   – end.